INTRODUCTION TO THE LAW OF CHRIST

F. BOURDEAU

A. DANET

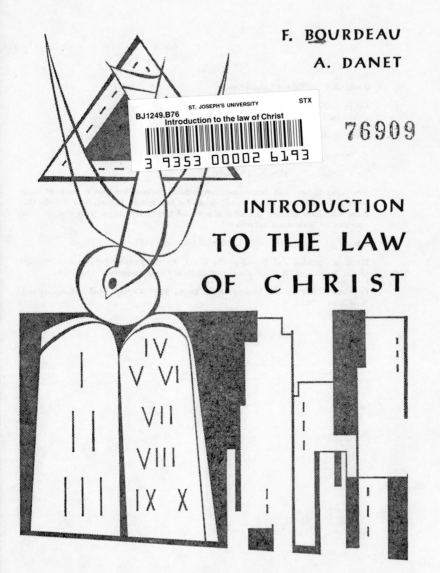

INTRODUCTION
TO THE LAW
OF CHRIST

Preface by Bernard Haring, C.Ss.R.

Translated by Edward Gallagher

Original title: Introduction à la Loi du Christ
published by Ligel, Paris

Nihil Obstat: John A. Goodwine, J.C.D., Censor Librorum

✠ Terence J. Cooke, D.D., V.G.

New York, N.Y.—February 17, 1966

The Nihil Obstat and Imprimatur are official declarations that a book or pamphlet is free of doctrinal or moral error. No implication is contained therein that those who have granted the nihil obstat and imprimatur agree with the contents, opinions or statements expressed.

Library of Congress Catalog Card Number: 66-16471

Designed, printed and bound in the U.S.A. by the Pauline Fathers and Brothers of the Society of St. Paul as a part of their Communications Apostolate.

CONTENTS

5

PREFACE

"Introduction to the Law of Christ." But who can introduce us into the beneficent kingdom of that law? In the last analysis, the triune God, and He alone. For to direct and introduce us to the Law of Christ means, in actual fact, to direct us to Christ Himself, to introduce us into His life and His love. Now He Himself testifies to this and insists upon it: "Therefore did I say to you, that no man can come to me, unless it be given him by my father" (John VI, 66). If He calls us to follow Him, He does so as the Son sent by the Father, while the most profound secret of His law, as He Himself enunciated it to His Apostles on a most solemn occasion, is the tremendous happening of Pentecost, the gift which He made to men of His Spirit on behalf of the Father. It is the work of the Spirit to lead us into all that Christ has told us because it is He who leads us into life and the love of Christ. And finally the miraculous inflowing of the Spirit is one with the work of the Father and of the Son: "My Father worketh until now; and I work" (John V, 17). "The Spirit of truth ... shall glorify me; because he shall receive of mine and shall show it to you. All things whatsoever the Father hath, are mine. Therefore I said that he shall receive of mine, and show it to you" (John XVI, 13, 14, 15). The mystery of the law of Christ is inherent in the mystery of the intra-Trinitarian relationship and in the divine mission in the world.

The law of the Lord is an interior, liberating and redemptive reality only for the man who, having been baptized in the Holy Spirit, utters a fundamental and decisive *yes* to the operation of the grace of that Spirit in him, as being the most authentic and most personal norm of his life. The law of Christ is essentially the "law of the spirit of life in Christ Jesus" (Rom. VIII, 2). The Spirit whom the Lord gives us desires to form the life of Jesus in us. He generates love in us, that love with which the Lord observed the Commandments, as He Himself said, as a mission received from His Father, that love which He imposed upon us as a law of grace (cf. John XV, 10-12). It is the work of the Spirit of love that we are no longer under a law felt as something extraneous, but that, free of all lawlessness, we have "in Christ," in a participation in the grace of His life and His love, our true law (I Cor. IX, 21).

The moral theologian's noble task, the task of those preaching on the moral teaching of the New Testament, as also of Christian parents and educators, is to introduce those in their care to the mystery of the law of Christ. But all human direction and introduction must remain vitally aware of the fact that it is the Spirit of the Lord Himself who in the last analysis performs that introduction. Moral theology and Christian moral pedagogy have no worth unless they humbly induce us to recognize the "law of the spirit of life in Christ Jesus," and to receive it with a grateful *yes*. It is from this starting point that the date and the fundamental structures of moral theology and Christian moral pedagogy are laid down, and so strongly brought into relief in the present work by my dear colleagues and valued collaborators, Fathers Bourdeau and Danet. May I be allowed to emphasize again, with them, the essential point.

Since nothing can separate us from the love of Christ unless we ourselves abandon that love (cf. Rom. VIII, 35),

8

so nothing in the whole world should be able to lead us to preach, in place of the mystery of the "law of the spirit of life in Christ Jesus," a moral code which consists of nothing more than precepts, commandments and prohibitions. In order to initiate men into this liberating mystery and to the joyous *yes* for which it calls, one could not bring too much devoted care to the task of marking the limitations of this definition of the obligatory minimum. Unhappy is he who, through laying too great stress upon legal rigorism and the superabundance of laws, so concentrates the attention of the Christian upon what is simply the exterior limit of his duty as to make him oblivious to Christ, and to His commandments of love and docility to the calls of grace of the Holy Spirit. The consequences flowing from this could be catastrophic, manifesting themselves either in a feeling of personal justice and hardness of heart based upon reliance on this code of exterior legal justice, or else in a refusal to accept the immutable designs of the Creator and Redeemer when presented in this guise.

We must thus avoid the temptation to seek to codify in the form of a legal limitation and to impose thus, as a purely external law, the "fruits of the Spirit," the "supererogatory works," and finally the demands, always new and inexhaustible, of the commandments of charity: "Be you therefore perfect, as also your heavenly Father is perfect" (Matt. V, 48). Our sole concern should be to introduce men with sweetness to the interior law of grace, to the free and joyous acceptance both of the general injunctions from which no one has the right to exempt oneself and to the particular invitations of grace.

The moralist theologian is always essentially the herald of the Good News of salvation. The prayer of the Apostle of the Gentiles he makes his own, as much for himself as

9

for those to whom he addresses himself; he makes it the soul of his teaching: "That the God of our Lord Jesus Christ the Father of glory, may give unto you the spirit of wisdom and of revelation, in the knowledge of him" (Eph. 1, 17). "That Christ may dwell by faith in your hearts; that being rooted and founded in charity, you may be able to comprehend, with all the saints, what is the breadth and the length, and height, and depth: to know also the charity of Christ, which surpasses all knowledge, that you may be filled unto all the fulness of God. Now to him who is able to do all things more abundantly than we ask for or understand, according to the power that worketh in us: to him be glory in the church, and in Christ Jesus . . ." (Eph. III, 17-21).

Moral theology is essentially the kerygma of the mystery of Christ, the kerygma of salvation, the joyous annunciation, filled with gratitude and praise, of the mighty works of God for us and in us. May this little book provide help to priests and educators in recognizing that more profoundly and realizing it joyfully. From first to last the aim is quite simply to lead men to a joyful and positive *yes* to the "law of the spirit of life." Part of the road towards this goal is to awaken their conscience to the feeling that we have not yet done enough in the quest for the Law of Christ, in the recognition of its sovereignty of charity and therefore of its demands.

B. Häring, C.Ss.R.
Rome, Alphonsian Institute.

10

Part I
Towards a morality based on the Mysteries of Christ

Before becoming involved in a detailed consideration of the fundamental principles of our Christian morality, would it not be advisable to have a look at it **in relation to bourgeois morality** and to the **existentialist and Marxist mystiques?** By doing this we should apprehend in lively fashion the fact of its originality (Chapter I).

It would be useful too to have a look at the subject in perspective by consulting the **history of moral theology.** There are many ways of examining and developing the requirements of Christian morality. History can help us to choose the best one (Chapter II).

The best route can only be Christ Himself. "I am the Way." **Our morality lies within** His Mystery. The whole course of our study, and even its plan, will derive from that for this **Mystery** is unfolded in **mysteries** (Chapter III).

CHAPTER ONE

CHRISTIAN MORALITY: ORIGINAL AND LIVING

"It is true that up to now the majority of treatises on morality continue to present a facade of dogged conservatism; yet the sound of cracking is beginning to make itself heard, and a new generation, from whom much may be expected, is appearing over the horizon." So said Canon Roger Aubert in 1954.[1]

Six years later Fr. Bernard Häring could confidently claim: "To-day under the influence of various determining factors, moral theology, in solid visible form, has begun to take its first steps."[2] Patched and plastered many times in the course of three centuries, the venerable edifice of the *Institutiones Morales* seemed at the very least to have gone out of plumb. Its views were in conflict with those of the liturgical, the biblical and the dogmatic revivals. Indeed there can no longer be any doubt about it—decrepit and ill-adjusted, it is finally admitting to the existence of chinks, it is sagging, and, like the classroom walls in Prévert's poem, is "crumbling peacefully."

▬▬▬▬▬▬▬▬▬▬▬

1. In *La théologie catholique au milieu de XXe siècle* (Ed. Casterman), p. 73.

2. In the course of a conference given in Paris in February 1960 under the presidency of Msgrs. E. Blanchet, R. Michon and J. Ménager. The complete text is to be found in the *Supplement à la Vie Spirituelle*, May 15, 1960, under the title "Renouveler la théologie morale? Pourquoi?" The phrase quoted, pp. 117-118.

There are some who will regret this. These "moral theologies" adroitly contrived the cohabitation of morality with the Law. So one had the impression of being able, thanks to them, to economize on a code of Canon Law, since all cases were already foreseen in them and solved down to the last detail. In reality what one was economizing on principally was the mystery of morality. For in this "concubinage" (the word is Fr. Häring's) the Law ended by arrogating to itself a supreme tyranny and making no secret of it any longer. "Many works proudly bore the title of 'Moral theology according to the norms of civil and canon law' or 'Moral theology in the light of canon and civil law.' It was not uncommon for legal casuistry to occupy nine-tenths of the contents.... And, what is even more serious, matters which strictly speaking are moral, including the sacraments, were themselves treated according to the method used in legal procedure which, as we all know, is chiefly concerned with defining the obligatory *minimum* in all circumstances (the legal minimum)."[3] Obviously the Holy Spirit had very little say in all of this, and the New Commandment, fraternal charity, made itself felt chiefly in the reminder that "true charity begins at home."

To-day it is vital to bring back the mystery of Christian morality into the full light of day. "Fear not, little flock." "He that followeth me, walketh not in darkness.... If any man thirst, let him come to me and drink... he that believeth in me." How many priests, when they recall certain regulations of Christian morality, have the feeling that they are defending the last redoubt. Let them now lift up their heads and consider the law of Christ, of which they are

3. Ibid., p. 120.

the heralds, in the pure light and clarity of the faith. *Confronted by the confusion of bourgeois morality, and by the mystiques of existentialism and Marxism,* this law will not appear antiquated to them, as the edifice which has been housing it might have led them to believe, but astonishingly current and original, fresh and new, like a source of living water leaping towards eternal life. "Our law is a law of grace" and not a catalogue of natural obligations. It is a *law of faith,* the outcome of a dialogue and a vital meeting with Jesus Christ. It is a *law of interior liberty* in the Spirit of Christ, and of *growing intercommunication,* for that Spirit is Love and His whole mission is to draw us all into the unity of the Trinity.

I. CONFRONT BOURGEOIS MORALITY WITH A MORALITY BASED UPON FAITH IN CHRIST

1. *"Nature" Moralists*

When all that is wanted is an "appeal to reason..."

A convenient but fallacious distinction often brings a radical misunderstanding into our conception of Christian morality....

Dogma, it is said, deals with God; morality, with man. All that is necessary is to harken to man's nature which dictates his ends to him; the Decalogue, it is made quite clear, does not go beyond the frontiers of the natural law. There is, of course, the Sermon on the Mount with its Beatitudes, but these are just simple exhortations to the best among us. Thus morality may be much more easily inculcated than dogma. It should be sufficient, in fact, to appeal to reason, to common sense. Everyone's conscience will bear out these assertions, will indeed instinctively anticipate them.

In spite of individual deviations, institutions which safeguard the common good will all have a common aim. There will hardly even be any need to consult reason—it will be enough to follow customs, traditions, good manners, the *proprieties* . . . .

And so, step by slippery step, the law of Christ falls to the level of bourgeois morality!

The weaknesses of a secular morality

Now let us see what is the worth of this equation which opens the doors to all sorts of moral weaknesses and lapses.

Simone de Beauvoir writes of her mother, the prisoner of a "stern traditionalist morality," who was introduced through her marriage into a milieu which was less strict: ". . . . she dreaded criticism and, in order to avoid it, took pains to 'be like everybody else.' In her new environment, her convent morality was only half-respected. She didn't want to be taken for a prude, and so she renounced her own standards of judgment: instead she decided that she would take the rules of etiquette as her guide."[4]

Of course these same rules of etiquette, shaped through the centuries of Christian civilization, do still preserve appearances to a certain extent, but, let us face it, to an ever-diminishing degree. And it is not secular morality which will save them.

"The fatal error of French radicalism," writes Gilson, referring to the taunts of Jean Paul Sartre, "lies in having wished to retain Christian morality, in having attempted to keep a society based on the Christian virtues without re-

---

4. In *Mémoires d'une jeune fille rangée,* Paris 1958, p. 40.

16

taining Christianity which alone had introduced these virtues into the world and alone can keep them alive .... The exact meaning of the famous 'secularism' is just that. It does not in any way indicate the creation of new values, for the secular spirit has invented nothing, but simply the secularization of Christian values. It is, to all intents and purposes, a claim to preserve the Christian values but free from the conditions which presided at their birth." And what is the result? "An atmosphere reeking with the decomposition of the corpse of a society having the form of Christianity from which all life has finally departed."[5]

▄▄▄▄▄▄▄▄▄▄▄▄▄▄▄

5. In *Pour un ordre catholique,* Paris 1934, pp. 41-44. Compare Jean Paul Sartre: "The existentialist is strongly opposed to a certain type of secular moralism which seeks to suppress God at the least possible expense. Towards 1880, when the French professors endeavored to formulate a secular morality, they said something like this: God is a useless and costly hypothesis, so we will do without it. However, if we are to have morality, a society and a law-abiding world, it is essential that certain values should be taken seriously; they must have an *a priori* existence ascribed to them. It must be considered obligatory *a priori* to be honest, not to lie, not to beat one's wife, to bring up children and so forth; so we are going to do a little work on this subject, which will enable us to show that these values exist all the same, inscribed in an intelligible heaven although, of course, there is no God. In other words— and this is, I believe, the purport of all that we in France call radicalism— nothing will be changed if God does not exist; we shall rediscover the same norms of honesty, progress and humanity, and we shall have disposed of God as an out-of-date hypothesis which will die away quietly of itself. The existentialist, on the contrary, finds it extremely embarrassing that God does not exist, for there disappears with Him all possibility of finding values in an intelligible heaven. There can no longer be any good *a priori,* since there is no infinite and perfect consciousness to think it. It is nowhere written that 'the good' exists, that one must be honest or must not lie, since we are now upon the plane where there are only men. Dostoievsky once wrote: 'If God did not exist, everything would be permitted;' and that, for existentialism, is the starting point." (*L'existentialisme est un Humanisme,* Paris 1946, pp. 34-36).

Let us be clear about this. What is left of bourgeois morality now? Well, the kind of thing whispered in my railway carriage the other day by a self-satisfied lady to a young mother struggling with a difficult baby: "Believe me, my dear, one child properly brought up is quite enough!"

Thorough decadence

If there is anyone who wants to find out, in this connection, the full claims of "reason" taking heed of "nature," he should consult Maurice Druon, the author of the well-known "Grandes Familles," "La Louve" and "Rois Maudits." In an article in *La Nef* entitled "L'Amour est à réinventer" ("Love must be re-invented"), he rejects, along with religious morality, bourgeois morality and secular morality, both of which still retain traces of religious morality, and he makes a plea for birth-control, for contraceptive techniques, for legalized abortion, artificial insemination, and, broadly speaking, for the separation of love from procreation. "Why must our customs and our laws continue to look with disfavor upon homosexuality?" And again, "obviously no one any longer seriously considers the principle of the indissolubility of marriage...." All that remains is simply to facilitate divorce, trial marriage and indeed free union. But what about the family? "It will disappear just as the tribe and the clan have disappeared in the case of primitive civilizations. Even the couple, considered as a social entity, no longer have any *raison d'être*."[6] The program is complete. All that it lacks is bestiality. In any case, it would be suf-

---

6. La Nef. Oct. - Nov. 1950, *L'Amour entre deux civilisations*, pp. 104-173.

ficient to call in Montherlant or Colette to fill in any gaps. And yet these people are intelligent; they are not anarchists or rebels. All they are doing is pleading in the name of reason for a natural liberty and an end to what, in their context, can be no more than taboos.

2. St. Paul, Christ's Moralist

What answer are we going to make to them?

Well, to start with, it is useless for us to take fright. St. Paul had to tackle a society no less corrupt than our own (cf. the first two chapters of the Epistle to the Romans!).

How does he expound morality to his Christians in Corinth, that celebrated maritime city open to all the sensual cults brought in from the East, tolerant of the vices of the young Roman tourists who came there on pleasure trips, indulgent to the love affairs of the sailors? "Meat for the belly and the belly for the meats" sniggered some of them (I Cor. VI, 13), and we may sense that they transposed this principle from gluttony to debauchery. Does Paul press his argument from the standpoint of reason? ... People should not eat all day long but according as the circumstances demand it, for we must eat to live and not live to eat. Equally, the sexual function should not be exercised indiscriminately, but with an eye to the wise propagation and training of life, for this function derives its primary meaning only when considered in relation to the preservation of the species.

Paul does not burden himself with this didactic approach. His logic is intuitive. If reason were based on nature then nature would instinctively have raised an obstacle to an abuse of itself; it would have been bound to suggest some *repulsion* in the face of lust, just as it does with drunkenness.

19

It is a fact, of course, that this reflex of natural prohibition may become dulled. But grace which perfects our nature will protect and strengthen this repugnance. Paul speaks to his people as Christians, and plays directly upon the incompatibility of this behavior *at the level of faith.* "You believe in Christ," he tells them; you are "joined to the Lord ... your bodies are the members of Christ. Shall I then take the members of Christ and make them the members of a harlot?" This is a shocking thought, horrifying, grotesque, impossible! Impossible according to the logic of the faith, according to the teaching Christians uphold. "Know you not that your members are the temple of the Holy Spirit, who is in you, whom you have from God; and you are not your own?" (I Cor. VI, 19-20).

When it is a question of marriage (Eph. V, 21-23), of lying (Eph. IV, 25) or of charity in general (all the Epistles), *Paul always bases his moral teaching on dogma.*[7] If he is preaching on the new life it is in terms of the resurrection of Christ, victory over corruption and over death, the central teaching of our faith. It is the mystery of Christ which shows clearly what is right for us and what is not. And that lesson is not only the most enlightening, it is also the most penetrating.

The love of Christ urges us more than anything else to follow His light (Eph. V, 1-2).

That's all very well, one may say, but how did he preach morality to unbelievers? The answer is, he did not preach morality to them. He told them of Christ.

----

7. Cf. A. Humbert, C.Ss.R., *La morale de saint Paul: morale du plan du salut,* in *Mélanges de Sciences religieuses,* 1958, pp. 5-44. Cf. also A. George, S.M., *La Morale de Paul,* Commission des Études Religieuses, 78, rue de Sèvres, Paris.

3. *Nature Transfigured by Grace*

It is Christ who reveals our sins to us; at the same time He reveals to us the assurance of forgiveness and our access to a higher dignity.

This is not to deny the natural law or to say that it is abolished by grace; but how much we can know of it with certainty in a world obscured by sin without the help of grace is not indeed very much. Even the philosophers admit this.

Etienne Gilson relates how as a young professor of philosophy in one of the state colleges he found himself entrusted with the teaching of morality to the junior and senior years. The headmaster whom he consulted on what bases to provide for this morality sent him along to the vice-principal, nicknamed "the bison," who put the emphasis on discipline: "Preach good conduct to them."

"I preached it. With what success we shall see. I had to return very soon to my vice-principal to ask him if he could not use his influence with my philosophy students who were 'escorted' every day right up to the door of the classroom where they were coming to learn morality with the object of obtaining the baccalaureat. His reply, an extremely sensible one, was that 'the girls did not come into the lycée' and that consequently 'it had nothing to do with anything.' In my innocence I asked him if he did not think it would be wise to advise the parents. And I got his second reply, no less shrewd than the first: 'They would say, "It's not contrary to nature, is it? Therefore it is natural."'

"I had just discovered the basis of morality."[8]

----

8. *Op. cit.*, p. 51.

What about Jacques Maritain's caution?

"The law and knowledge of the law are two different things," he writes. "The natural law is not a written law . . . . It is written, so it is said, in the heart of man. True, but in the hidden depths, as hidden from us as the heart itself . . . . Men recognize it with greater or less difficulty, and in differing degrees, and always in danger of error here as in other matters. The only practical knowledge which all men have naturally and with certainty in common is that they should do good and avoid evil . . . . Montaigne observed with some malice that to certain peoples incest and theft were regarded as virtuous actions, which scandalized Pascal.

"The knowledge which our own moral conscience has of this law is undoubtedly imperfect too, and it is probable that it will keep on developing and refining so long as human nature lasts. When the Gospel has penetrated to the very depths of the substance of human nature the natural law will appear in its full flower and perfection."[9]

The First Vatican Council ratified this teaching, for it also has moral knowledge in view when it says: "It must be attributed to divine revelation that certain facts, in themselves accessible to human reason concerning divine things, can be known in the present condition of the human race, *ab omnibus expedite, firma certitudine et nullo admixto errore*[10] (easily by all, with firm and unerring certainty). Showing man his way includes knowledge of divine things

----

9. In *Les droits de l'homme et la loi naturelle,* Paris 1945, pp. 65-66.

10. Cf. Denziger 1786. On the respective functions of moral philosophy and moral theology in respect of the natural law cf. Ph. Delhaye, *Le droit natural, recherches historiques et doctrinales,* especially the pedagogical aspects, in *L'Ami du Clergé,* April 14, 1960, pp. 225-228.

because man is "capable of dialogue with God" and because in God alone can he find rest and peace. Even left to his nature alone his dignity would be intelligible to him, he would be intelligible to himself only as one drawn towards that ideal which completes his nature by transfiguring it; as one to whom God speaks and proposes an ineffable friendship. But he knows himself clearly to be capable of dialogue only when God Himself takes the initiative and calls him. Then he realizes the true dignity of his nature, and that he was capable of becoming wholly and with every aspect of his being "a response to God." *Agnosce o christiane, dignitatem tuam.* (Know, O Christian, your own dignity). This means that morality does not speak solely of man, but of man as he stands in his relationship to God. Why should it be surprising that those who deny God misunderstand themselves?

"This is the victory .... our faith"

Sinners as we are we can know our nature only in the transfiguration of the divine friendship, in the light of faith, and also, therefore, in the *obedience required by faith.* For here on earth the faith makes us subject to the conscience of the Church protected by an infallible magisterium. The center of reference for our morality is not the reason of each man ratified by the common sense of all men; it is the faith of the Church, that is to say, the intelligence of believers enlightened by faith. Through it the risen Christ calls upon us and reveals to us what we really are, and how we must be united to Him *through love.* Our moral fidelity to the dignity of our nature is a victory over the corruption of the world. And our victory is always our faith. "For this

23

is the charity of God, that we keep his commandments: and his commandments are not heavy. For whatsoever is born of God, overcometh the world: and this is the victory which overcometh the world, our faith" (I John, V, 3-4).

Suppose that tomorrow the government were to propose two kinds of marriage: the one a simple, straightforward contract of association which could be dissolved easily as soon as one of the partners were to lapse on one of the clauses of the contract, or were to want the contract broken; the other to be as indissoluble as the bonds of blood. It is obvious that Christians, under pain of betraying their faith, could enter only the second kind of marriage. They would do so conscious that by this they were fulfilling the wishes of nature whose carnal condition may not express the absolute of love except by an exclusive giving which cannot be withdrawn; but Christians possess the assurance of this absolute of love through faith in Christ which overcomes the jibes and skepticism of unbelievers. Thus too they should appear, through the very marriage they would choose, as a "sign" of the ineffable gift which God has given to us in Christ, a sign of the indissoluble love of Christ for His Church .... To counter a crumbling bourgeois morality perhaps we might adopt this standpoint, as old as St. Paul (Eph. V, 31-32), and so much plainer, franker and more vigorous than all the reasonings of nature! The Christian is that odd character who chooses to spend his life swimming against the stream of what is generally accepted, and is aware of it because he is dealing with his nature in the light of Christ. *In a world which is the slave of pseudo-proprieties, his law is Christ* (I Cor. IX, 21). He belongs to Christ. He lives by faith in the resurrection in Christ. "Who is he that overcometh the world, but he that believeth that Jesus is the Son of God?" (I John, V, 5).

II. COUNTER EXISTENTIALISM WITH A MORALITY OF INTERIOR FREEDOM

1. *Liberty without Law*

Does not such a claim, which makes our morality dependent upon faith, put it in a somewhat delicate position when brought face to face with the contemporary mystiques of liberty? We have freed ourselves from the insipid morality of the proprieties but only so that we may serve God on an even narrower basis. St. Paul says so; there is no question of gainsaying that: "... we have been made servants of justice" (Rom. VI, 18). Were we free? Well, behold us now, become "servants ... of Christ" (Eph. VI, 5); "servants of God" (I Peter, II, 16).

Opposing this "morality of servitude," existentialism announces to men the terrifying news, the good news of their total, agonizing and exciting *liberty*. It impugns even the basis of the natural law. There is neither Good nor Evil, with capital letters, neither God nor Devil; there is nothing save man.

"Man, condemned to be free"

Fearful news this, for then man is abandoned, in complete dereliction. Simone de Beauvoir, when she expunged God from her life, felt it as a brutal experience:

"... I felt with anguish the emptiness of heaven. Until then, I had stood at the center of a living tableau whose colors and lighting God Himself had chosen; all things murmured softly of His glory. Suddenly everything fell silent. And what a silence! The earth was rolling through space that was unseen by any eye, and lost on its immense surface, there I stood alone, in the midst of the sightless regions of the air. Alone: for the first time I understood the terrible significance of that word. Alone: without a witness, without anyone to speak to, without refuge."[11]

But wonderful emancipation! There was no longer any restriction, no longer any judge. There were no longer any norms and everything was in confusion.

"I lost no time in embracing the principles of immoralism. Of course, I did not approve of people stealing out of self-interest or going to bed with someone for the pure pleasure of it; but if these became quite gratuitous acts, acts of desperation and revolt—and, of course, quite imaginary—I was prepared to stomach all the vices, the rapes and the assassinations you might care to mention ... there is not much distance between a super-human sacrifice and a gratuitous crime, and I saw in Sygne the sister of Lafcadio."[12]

Literary immoralism? Well, Sartre was soon, in his "Saint Genêt, comédien et martyr" to vindicate vices as little imaginary as the prison which they earned for their skilled practitioner. Sartre laid down his theory, too, with plenty of logic:

"And when we speak of 'abandonment'—a favorite word of Heidegger—we only mean to say that God does not exist, and that it is necessary to draw the consequences of his absence right to the end.... Dostoievsky once wrote 'If God did not exist, everything would be permitted;' and that for existentialism, is the starting point. Everything is indeed permitted if God does not exist, and man is in consequence forlorn, for he cannot find anything to depend upon either within or outside himself. He discovers forth-

11. *Mémoires d'une jeune fille rangée,* p. 139.
12. *Ibid.,* pp. 194-195.

with, that he is without excuse. For if indeed existence precedes essence, one will never be able to explain one's action by reference to a given and specific human nature; in other words, there is no determinism—man is free, man *is* freedom. Nor, on the other hand, if God does not exist, are we provided with any values or commands that could legitimize our behavior. Thus we have neither behind us, nor before us in a luminous realm of values, any means of justification or excuse. We are left alone, without excuse. That is what I mean when I say that man is condemned to be free."[13]

No more natural law, only situations

You have read aright; there is no nature. One can no longer dream of the certain emancipation of the natural law. The very world which surrounds us is only a contingent and provisional ordering of things, wholly devoid of meaning outside of any which we freely give to it. This is what is expresesd by the well-known ravings of Roquentin, in *La Nausée,* when he surveys from his vantage point on the hill the "charming bourgeois city" where people feel so secure this evening, but where cunning existence creeps and prowls, preparing a witches' sabbath in the style of Hieronymus Bosch!

"... They have proof, a hundred times a day, that everything happens mechanically, that the world obeys fixed, unchangeable laws. In a vacuum all bodies fall at the same rate of speed, lead melts at 335 degrees centigrade, the last streetcar leaves the Hôtel de Ville at 11:05 p.m. ... And all this time, great vague nature has slipped into their

13. In *L'existentialisme est un humanisme,* Paris 1946, pp. 33-37.

city.... I *see* it, I *see* this nature.... I know that its obedience is idleness, I know it has no laws: ... what they take for constancy is only habit and it can change tomorrow.

"... A mother might look at her child's cheek and ask him: 'What's that? A pimple?' and see the flesh puff out a little, split, open, and at the bottom of the split an eye, a laughing eye might appear.... And someone else might feel something scratching in his mouth... and his tongue is an enormous live centipede, rubbing its legs together and scraping his palate.... Men all alone... will run through the streets,... their eyes staring, fleeing their ills yet carrying them with them, open-mouthed, with their insect-tongue flapping its wings.... Then I'll burst out laughing.... I'll lean against a wall and when they go by I'll shout: 'What's the matter with your science? What have you done with your humanism? Where is your dignity?' "[14]

Let us be serious! Existentialism is indeed humanism, but without an order determined by God. Everything changes. There are only general *situations* subject to evolution, and, concretely, historical situations in which we are embroiled, involved, and which require our decisions. It is necessary to take sides in this entanglement, to opt, to choose. It is up to every individual to find his own response on every occasion. For we are free. Whoever denies that is deceiving himself. And whoever refuses to find his own route is in bad faith. In the name of what should one choose, since there is neither Good nor Evil, since there are no values? In the name of liberty itself.

"... the actions of men of good faith have, as their ultimate significance, the quest of freedom itself as such....

14. In *La Nausée* by J. P. Sartre, Paris 1938, pp. 198-200, *passim*.

We will freedom for freedom's sake, and in and through particular circumstances."[15]

And by the same token everyone wills the freedom of others with whom his own freedom is involved.

"And in thus willing freedom, we discover that it depends entirely upon the freedom of others and that the freedom of others depends upon our own."[16]

A question which arises

A certain question arises here concerning that freedom of others. Do I want it so that I shall enjoy my freedom, or so that they shall enjoy theirs? In the first instance this vindication of liberty is only one more variation on the old egoistic eudemonism. In the second instance liberty is no longer an empty thing—it aims at improving the lot of others through motives of disinterested love. But then, *if human love does not abolish liberties, if it is listed among them as something appealing, why should the love of God destroy them?*

For atheistic existentialism does not advance any proof of the non-existence of God. It decrees it, *a priori*. If God were to exist He would hamper our liberties. But if our human liberties are of strength to one another when they meet, what should happen when our human liberties meet the divine liberty? And if we are moving essentially towards that meeting, must we not choose it before all else?[17]

▪▪▪▪▪▪▪▪▪▪▪▪▪▪

15. In *L'existentialisme est un humanisme* by J. P. Sartre, Paris 1946, p. 82.

16. *Ibid.*, p. 83.

17. Cf. J. Daniélou, *Scandaleuse vérité*, chap. II, Vérité et liberté, p. 29-42.

Consider the contemptible ignorance displayed by F. Jeanson when he allows himself to muse ironically:

"If God exists the fact is that he never asked our opinion before plunging us into this turmoil in which we find ourselves. If he really has the intention and the means to save us, one may suppose that in such a matter he will succeed by himself. And if he has omitted to let us know his plans we are not even able to help him."[18]

This is precisely the opposite of what faith in Jesus Christ teaches, namely that God, having created us by Himself does not want to save us by Himself; He respects too much the liberty which He has given to us.

2. *A Law of Liberty*

Are we not, unfortunately, responsible to some extent for this misunderstanding of the situation? If there was one truth which our classic manuals left in the dark it is surely this one, that *our morality is a morality of liberation and of liberty*.

"For the law of the spirit of life in Christ Jesus, hath delivered me from the law of sin and of death" (Rom. VIII, 2). St. Paul has no more cherished idea. "Servants of Christ?" We realize that this is an antiphrasis. This servitude of love is the supreme liberty. "For he that is called in the Lord, being a bondman, is the freeman of the Lord . . . be not made the bondslaves of men" (I Cor. VII, 22-23). Paul dares to say: ". . . you are not *under the law,* but under grace" (Rom. VI, 14); not so much *"without law,"* but "in the law of Christ" (I Cor. IX, 21). The *"law of liberty,"*

---

18. In *Sartre par lui-même,* Paris 1955, p. 180.

St. James calls it (II, 12), *"the perfect law of liberty"* (I, 25).

Here we are at the very heart of the mystery of Christian morality.

Liberty lies in communion

Man, in fact, is free. God has made him a lord in His own image. It was not his work to create forms of life, subject to slow changes. But he found them, classified them, "invented" new arrangements of them. Adam named the animals. Man orders, that is to say he both disposes and commands. He makes the universe speak. Man is in fact the one who gives human significance to things. In whose service should he exercise this domination? For his own egoistic benefit? Not at all. God did not judge it good that he should live alone. While he savors his liberty through exploration, work and the contemplation of nature in a proper dialogue and companionship with things, *man expands that liberty only in encounter with others,* in the free recognition of other liberties and above all in the free acknowledgement of God to whom he relates the universe as the gift God has made to him. (That this acknowledgement is free the frantic denial of the existentialists proves clearly enough for us!) Thus *nature and natural things appear to provide the point where liberties encounter one another in exchange and communion.* We believe in natural things but they must be subordinated to liberties. Man is that being who is capable of transmuting all the natural conditions into a matter of free choice. Man is a person, someone who is called to make of values and natural things *a meeting-place for the encounter with others.*

A liberty which becomes servitude

The weakness lies in wanting to halt at the natural things, wanting to corner them for oneself, or loving others with a narrow love which is secretly vitiated by egoism and the rejection of universal communion—the egoism of a people, or of a group, or the egoism of two people, which is no less anti-social than solitary passion. By acting thus man begins to pervert the natural things, has indeed already perverted them by the fact that he no longer subordinates them to universal communication. Lacking this he stifles, becomes atrophied, demands more and more of the natural things to fill at all costs that void which they cannot fill, and is dominated by their tyrannical attraction. Whoever claims to live thus, in a mortuitous manner, to "live his life in complete liberty," is settling down into chaos, contradiction and death, into which he plunges all things by refusing to make them serve this encounter of liberties. Exposed to the accusing Law, he is the prisoner of his own false happiness, and already dead, since he knows that this temporary satisfaction is going to perish. He is a servant of his sin, a servant and not free.

A servitude which is liberty

But "the grace of God by Jesus Christ our Lord ... the law of the spirit of life ... hath delivered (you) from the law of sin and of death" (Rom. VII, 25; VIII, 2). Through the mystery of the Resurrection Christ places our corporal nature itself within the sphere of the Spirit; it can no longer help but serve the encounter of people. And He actually gives us a share in this vivifying Spirit. We have only to follow His inspirations, His suggestions and we shall be free.

Our law is the Holy Spirit, or, in other words, supreme liberty. We do not have to live according to a paralyzing code, a stifling strait-jacket of precepts and customs as under the Old Law. We live according to the breath of the Spirit.

"The essential in the law of the New Testament, and in this lies its strength, is that it is the grace of the Holy Spirit which is given through faith in Christ. And so the New Law is principally (*principaliter*) the grace of the Holy Spirit Himself."[19]

Our morality is for ever liberated from an ideal of conformity to some exterior law, by obeying which one would be justified. But we are in fact subject to Another. Is it not a strange paradox then to talk of liberty? It is not strange if this Other has become Ours. It is not strange if the secret of liberty is a secret of love and reciprocal indwelling. "And I live, now not I, but Christ liveth in me" (Gal. II, 20). He has given me His Spirit which is not the spirit of bondage but the spirit of adoption of sons and of filial liberty (cf. Rom. VIII, 15). I live in the faith of Christ, and simultaneously I do what I want. I live according to my own taste, to my own fashion, because it is Christ whom I love. My spirit is His! St Thérèse of Lisieux used to say: "I always do my own will." And not only a finite and poverty-stricken will. Because the Love of God dwells in me and Christ lives in me my will is mystically identified with that of the Creator of heaven and earth. I am free with a sovereign liberty: "Mine are the heavens and mine the earth ... for Christ is mine and wholly for me" (St. John of the Cross).

"*All things are lawful to me,* I can say with St. Paul

––––––––––––––––––

19. In St. Thomas, S.T., Ia IIae, q. 106, a. 1. Cf. S. Lyonnet, *Liberté chrétienne et loi de l'Esprit selon saint Paul,* in *Christus,* Oct. 1954, p. 6.

33

(I Cor. VI, 12); I have only my own law to follow, that of the Holy Spirit who is in Christ. I fulfill the will of another and I am free, I do my own will which God has cast in His mold. The Christian acts according to the law of his own being and of his life, which is the law of his heart. He does what he loves to do. For the law of life, inscribed in the risen Christ and inscribed in our hearts is the Law of the Spirit of Life (Rom. VIII, 12) and the Spirit of God is the love of God distributed in our hearts. To fulfill the will of God it is sufficient for the Christian to follow his own love." [20]

Beyond casuistry

This is why casuistry will never be the sum of our morality. It is indeed to be found on the side of a morality of essences, indispensable but inadequate. In a word it is each individual liberty which knows all that the love of Christ demands of it in each situation. Christ calls each of us by his own name (John X, 3), each of us must follow his calling, the calling of life and the calling of every day of life. He must—not within the general commandments, it is true but beyond—find his own response of love to the Love of Christ. It is from this side that a true Christian formula of the false "ethics of the situation" must be sought. It will not be an invitation to laxity but to a life wholly given over to the authentic inspiration of the gifts of the Holy Spirit.

▄▄▄▄▄▄▄▄▄▄▄▄▄▄▄

20. In F. X. Durrwell's *Sainteté chrétienne, sainteté d'obéissance*, in *La Vie Spirituelle*, Oct. 1956, p. 268. Cf. M. Zundel: "We are here, then, as far from the heteronomy of an order which would remain quite exterior to us as from the claimed autonomy of a law which our will would alone be given" (*Le poème de la Sainte Liturgie*, p. 106).

3. *The Fight For Liberty*

The conquest of liberty

The foregoing is all very well, it may be said, but none-
theless the Commandments must be obeyed. Am I free if
I cannot free myself from them when they weigh upon me?
Wait a minute! When the love of Christ weighs upon you,
it is then that you are not free. A pseudo-liberation from
the demands of this love would serve but to strengthen your
slavery. But it is only too true that we are not fully risen
with Christ. "For we know that the law is spiritual; but
I am carnal, sold under sin" (Rom. VII, 14). So, note,
"... you have been called unto liberty: only make not
liberty an occasion to the flesh, but by charity of the spirit
serve one another" (Gal. V, 13). "For we know that every
creature groaneth and travaileth in pain even till now. And
not only it, but ourselves also, who have the first fruits
of the Spirit, even we ourselves groan within ourselves,
waiting for ... the redemption of our body" (Rom. VIII,
22-23).

Obedience, the school of liberty

"We are not yet entirely dead to ourselves nor totally
governed by God. Our submission being still imperfect,
our liberty is also incomplete. Only in heaven shall we
have nothing more to do than follow the law of our hearts,
of the Spirit, who will then be our only principle of life.
In the meantime ... it is necessary that the will of God
be intimated to us from outside too, through the Church
and her innumerable institutions, the hierarchy, Canon Law,
particular religious laws. All these institutions are provi-

35

sional, of value during our terrestrial pilgrimage, while our imperfections persist, until we shall attain 'unto the measure of the age of the fulness of Christ' (Eph. IV, 13)." [21]

Between now and then we must live "with Christ . . . nailed to the cross" in order to share in His resurrection (Gal. II, 19); that is to say, "crucify the flesh and its vices and concupiscences" (Gal. V, 24) for which purpose obedience to the precepts which we find difficult is useful because it puts us on the same footing with the obedience of Christ on the cross (Phil. II, 8). *So far from being in opposition to liberty, it is, in fact, an introduction to it.* Christian obedience is the personal school of liberty. God respects our liberty so much that He wishes us to make the conquest of it ourselves. Hence we must aim to make our obedience like that of Christ, a free sacrifice, a supreme oblation of our liberty.

A significant admission

Here we are, you will say, back again to the struggle, back to sacrifices! And you feel inclined to throw a surreptitious glance—oh, just the merest flick of a nostalgic eye upon the pure, the simple, the absolute liberty of which the existentialists would appear to possess the secret and the prerogative. You may rest easy. They have finally admitted that they have no secret at all and no prerogatives either. This wonderful morality of free man which Sartre promised us—it is possible now that he will never describe it, for now he is rejoining Marxism—this liberty does not exist. There has to be a struggle to win it.

"As soon as there shall exist *for all* a margin of real

---

21. F. X. Durrwell, art. cit., p. 269.

liberty beyond the production of life, Marxism will be dead; a philosophy of liberty will take its place. But we have no method, no intellectual instrument, no concrete experience which allows us to conceive this liberty, nor this philosophy."[22]

When we can do this, when all egoism has disappeared from the hearts of men we shall be in heaven!

III. COUNTER MARXISM WITH A MORALITY OF TRUE CHARITY

1. *Fraternity Without Morality*

Marxism, for Sartre, is the philosophy of the epoch, and existentialism has no ambition to be other than an *ideology* to be used in its service for the analysis of concrete problems.[23]

Apparent success

This time Christian morality, the morality of the Beatitudes, the morality of Heaven, is surely going to have to admit that it is stripped of much. Confronted by the marvels of this revolutionary mystique which has been able to con-

---

22. In *Critique de la raison dialectique* by J. P. Sartre, t. 1. Paris 1960, p. 32.

23. *Ibid.*, passim; for instance, "Marxism remains therefore the philosophy of our times; it cannot be got over because the circumstances which have brought it about are not yet got over" (p. 29). Or again in a letter to Roger Garaudy: "Marxism as a formal framework of all philosophic thought of today cannot be transcended," quoted by R. Garaudy, *Perspectives de l'homme*, Paris 1960, p. 112.

vulse peoples and make the whole world tremble, grappling directly with history and progress, this mystique which may be in the course of a successful attempt at the totalitarian socialization of the entire planet, our words of mercy and of charity must surely seem lacking in vigor, sharp outline, éclat, must appear too sweet, too mawkish, too colorless.

To be sure, Marxist morality is inhuman. Or rather, let us say, Marxism which has set itself up in dogmatic form, has cut down on morality. But should one not recognize in its "praxis," in its concrete action to change social conditions and to promote—in due course—a society which is more just and more human, a sensational effectiveness? *Is it not building a fraternal community without morality?*

Shadows on the picture

Let us take precautions right from the beginning against a kind of mythological confusion. The major part of the effectiveness which we are tempted to recognize in Marxism *as such*, derives from the fact that it has been working hand in hand with the economic success and claim to world hegemony of the Soviet Union. This is no more astonishing in itself than the success in one century, and parallel hegemony, of the United States, and in actual fact requires no more fundamental explanation than that of the historic encounter between industrial and scientific progress and a territory endowed with enormous resources in raw material, up to then, by force of circumstances, unexploited. This said, let us recognize in its preaching of a humanitarian gospel and the hope of social upheaval an undeniable radiance which captivated the underdeveloped peoples, but let us realize immediately that these are Christian ideals which, deprived of spiritual dimension, become unbalanced and

38

even, alas, lethal. *That fraternity without morality could well be used for the establishment of an empire without fraternity.* In reality our Christian morality has nothing to fear when confronting Marxism, but Marxism ought to be for us an urgent invitation to give back to our Gospel all the vigor of its revolutionary ferment.

2. A Morality of Fraternity

When one betrays Christian morality

Alas, and again alas! Where in our classic manuals are the treatises on human hope? What role is played in them by fraternal charity? And the Beatitudes? When we make the promise of heaven only to those who hunger and thirst after justice, are we sure that we are not making it unattractive and dull? Have we forgotten the mighty words of St. Paul proclaiming that there is no longer either Jew or Greek, bond or free, but that in Christ, the true "new Man," we are all "a new creation," the citizens of a new world? And when we see St. Paul specifically pleading for the forgiveness of Onesimus, a fugitive servant—"... receive him as a most dear brother ... receive him as myself" (Philemon 16-17)—can we possibly believe that this liberty, this equality, this spiritual fraternity does not belong naturally to the temporal condition of men?

Do we realize the harm which could have been done to us by the odious principles which Marx was able to read in a Catholic paper and which he recorded as "the social principles of Christianity?"

"Poverty is the lot of a section of society. This is a law of God to which we do well to submit.

"Society has need of servants, it cannot continue except

at whatever this costs. It is necessary that there be men who work a great deal and who live wretchedly.

"Resign yourselves to laborious poverty and you will receive your reward and eternal compensation."[24]

Fraternal charity, the center of morality

Is it in heaven that Christ wants us to love one another, to receive the poorest, and also to give our coats?

Charity is His new commandment, His central commandment, and we need not be afraid to call it *fraternal* charity—how fraternal the following texts unequivocally show. This charity does not exist if it is not participation through grace in the same love with which God loves us, but it is as fraternal charity that it is at the center of our morality.

Is it really possible to construct our whole morality in the form of a deployment of the demands of fraternal charity? Yes, St. Paul himself traces the plan of it perfectly simply when he writes: "For he that loveth his neighbor hath fulfilled the law." In fact he expressly adds: "For thou shalt not commit adultery: Thou shalt not kill: Thou shalt not steal: Thou shalt not bear false witness: and if there be any other commandment, it is comprised in this word: Thou shalt love thy neighbor as thyself.... Love of our neighbor ... therefore is the culmination of the law" (Rom. XIII, 8-10).

Theologians themselves have even acknowledged in this connection:

"When one bethinks oneself of the extension of charity

----

24. *L'Univers* of July 7, 1848, quoted by G. Fessard in *France, prends garde de perdre ta liberté*, 1946, p. 303.

to one's neighbor, and how this extension does not shatter the unity of the theological virtue, does not one come to ask oneself if fraternal charity should not also rank as one of the theological virtues? Theologians, to our knowledge, have not discussed this question."[25]

This must be the work of our time. All the commandments bearing upon the Christian will appear as mediations of fraternal charity, through the intervention, especially, of the virtue of justice, in such a way that this virtue will be truly irradiated by charity and that it will be conceived as responsible not only for the just disposition of benefits in the existing economic order, but dedicated to promoting an ever better order and a society ever more fraternal.

3. *Truth, Liberty, Fraternity*

The fallacy of Marxist materialism

Christians must always be in the front ranks of this fight, but they must wage it with their own weapons, and with the object of setting up a society other than a Marxist society, for this, resting as it does upon the dictatorship of violence, gives every indication of being one of the most colossal impostures of history, producing a world of lies, of terror and of hatred, constructed in the name of scientific truth, integrity and fraternity.

The most subtle temptation of Marxism really lies not in its evangelism but in its *materialism*.

Dostoievsky's *Legend of the Grand Inquisitor* should be continuously re-read. What Marxism is proposing to human-

25. P. Deman, O.P., *La charité fraternelle, forme des vertus,* in *La Vie spirituelle,* 1946, p. 392.

ity is *the security of a human slave.* Fill us with bread, and that will do! The mystique of "the good earth," the rejection of the spiritual adventure and of the divine confrontation, has a disintegrating effect upon everything; even human relations are robbed of their spiritual dimension. And material satiety will very shortly produce its own fruit, disgust and death, for man does not live by bread alone.

The strength of Christian morality

The strength of Christian morality, but also its essential requirement, is that it possesses both *liberty* and *fraternity* in the *truth* of Christ. It refuses to claim to establish fraternity by new alienations. It believes in the interior liberty of every individual face to face with God Himself. And it does not simply add up to these two principles, *it combines them.* Contrary to an over-simplistic and illusory image, it does not consider that the relationship with God is vertical and the relationship with others is horizontal, and both of them exteriorizing. It considers that both are interior.[26] For God is in me more myself than I am, and true fraternity is primarily interior. It is in the conquest of true liberty through charity towards God that true liberty towards one's neighbor is affirmed, which is true fraternity. For each and for both the principle is, Christ in us, our law. "For the law of the spirit of life, in Christ Jesus, hath delivered me from the law of sin and of death" (Rom. VIII, 2) and

---

26. "It is in the supreme interiority of our will that we give ourselves to Another who is more interior to us than ourselves. What, in any case, is more interior to a person than his love and the object of his love" (M. Zundel, *op. cit.*, p. 106). We shall utilize this scheme only in reference to time and eternity, cf. p. 85).

this is why you are able to hear the joyful news: "Bear ye one another's burdens; and so you shall fulfill the law of Christ" (Gal. VI, 2).

Such is our morality, stronger and more real than any other, provided that it is recaptured truly in its mystery, that is, in the Mystery of Christ.

CHAPTER TWO

THE LESSON TO BE LEARNED FROM A HISTORY OF MORAL THEOLOGY

While plenty of research has been done during the last fifty years into the history of dogmas, moralists long neglected to write the history of morality. Today, however, they seem to have decided to make up for their tardiness; monographs are appearing on all sides; light is being shed on obscure periods; and already important lessons are emerging.

Without fear of later contradiction one can emphasize the fact that the chief lesson which emerges is that *moral theology is bound up with dogma* and neither progresses nor expands unless and until it recognizes this bond. The vicissitudes of its history correspond with periods when attempts were made to divorce the two. There is evidence of this in each of the epochs, that of the Fathers, the Scholastic period and the modern era. In this survey we shall, of course, indicate only some of the main points along the route.

I. THE PERIOD OF THE FATHERS: LIFE IN CHRIST

1. *The Unity of Dogma and Morality in the new Christian existence*

"When it is a question of marriage (Eph. V, 21-23), of lying (Eph. IV, 25) or of charity in general," as we have said, "Paul always rests his moral lessons on dogma." [1]

So too, in his wake, did the *Fathers*, to the point that they do not even draw a distinction between dogma and morality, truths to believe and commandments to practice. For them Christianity is a *mystery to be lived*, the mystery of the imitation of the divine principles of Jesus Christ.

Apologists

For the Apologist Fathers of the second century, the moral conduct of Christians, so different from the dissolute behavior and principles of the society which surrounded them, was but the logical consequence of their new life in Christ. *The change of morals assumes the change of faith and is an indication of authenticity.* Let us listen to St. Justin:

"From the time we came to believe in the Word we renounced the cult of the devil in order to attach ourselves through the Son of God alone and uncreated. Formerly we took pleasure in debauchery; today it is chastity which delights us.... We loved and sought money and lands more than all else; today we pool everything we have and we share with the poor. Hatreds and crimes divided us...; today after the coming of Christ, we live together, we pray for our enemies, we endeavor to win over our unjust persecutors." [2]

Without a doubt no one has ever found a better formula for the mutual inclusion of dogma and morality in Christian-

----

1. See above, p. 20.
2. Justin, in *Apolog.*, XIV, 2-3.

ity than did the author of the Epistle to Diognetus (end of second century):

"There is no life without learning and no sure learning without the true Life.... Let learning become identified with feeling, let the Word of Truth received in you become your life."[3]

Martyrs and Monks

Why were so many Christians able to face martyrdom? Why did such a large number of them retire to the desert to lead that monastic life which in the Church, as we know, has taken on the force of martyrdom. The answer is because of their living faith in the precept "follow the Lord," because as St. Ignatius of Antioch expressed it, they wanted to "imitate the Passion of their God."[4]

Mystagogues

Every Christian is called to participate in this Passion through the sacraments. For the great writers of the 4th and 5th centuries, the majority of those pastors and catechists like St. Cyril of Jerusalem or St. Hilary of Poitiers, all the moral conduct of Christians originates in the fact that we are divinized by faith and the sacraments. For the most part their teaching could be searched in vain for any moral treatise properly so-called: their moral teaching is not autonomous, it is almost always *bound up with the*

---

3. *To Diognetus* XII, 4 and 7.
4. Ignatius in *Letter to the Romans*, VI; cf. *Letter to the Magnesians*, V. Cf. L. Bouyer, *La Spiritualité du N. T. et des Pères* (Paris 1960), p. 238 et seq.

mystagogical teaching which accompanies the liturgy of the Christian assembly.

2. *The Primacy of the Christian Message over the Findings of Philosophy*

The Fathers were not ignorant of the Greek conceptions, the influence of which on later Judaism was already discernible. Nevertheless in the arch of their wisdom the keystone always remains bedded in the Christian revelation, not in nature.

Clement and Origen

The scholars of Alexandria, Clement and shortly afterwards Origen, both men of high culture and very much *au fait* with the ideas and aspirations of their time, tried to integrate without either reservation or timidity the best of Greek thought with the Christian revelation. But they too are quite explicit: *Christian morality has only one explanation,* namely Christ, "the Teacher par excellence," as Clement calls Him.[5] The life of the Christian, who is the image of God, is an imitation of God in Jesus Christ. From this firm conviction they even proceeded to the bold and sanguine conclusion that if certain pagans were noteworthy for a life of superior quality, this was because in fact the *Logos* of God, Christ, was present incognito and at work in their hearts. A moral life of high quality can only be explained through Christ.

----

5. Clement of Alexandria in *Le Pédagogue.* See introduction by H. I. Marrou (Collection "Sources chrétiennes," Paris 1960).

Saint Ambrose

The first attempt to systematize Christian morality must be credited to St. Ambrose. He called it very simply *De Officiis*, the actual title of a Ciceronian treatise which he "baptized" to convert it into a kind of moral directory for the use of his clerics. Thus there entered into our theology the four cardinal virtues, a classification of Stoic origin. Such borrowing was interesting for the period; perhaps there is far too little of it done today.[6]

Saint Augustine

Another disciple of Cicero, the rhetorician Augustine, could not have failed to borrow from the eclectic philosophy of the period. For instance, the Stoics believed in a pneuma, an interior, invisible force, pervading the world and maintaining it in cohesion and unity. St. Augustine draws from this the concept of *the natural law* placed by God in the heart of created man. This is a definitive acquisition to our thought provided that we bear in mind that this concept may have subsequently become secularized and congealed into an impersonal idea. For the author of the *Confessions* the natural law resounds at the level of conscience in each one of us, and conscience is the voice of God—a God whose designs of love are revealed to us by faith. No one has better succeeded in drawing profit from the biblical inheritance of *man in dialogue with his Creator,* man haunted by the divine Mercy and yet tempted to answer 'No' to its appeals. As a convert he saw and lived Christianity as a

6. Cf. Ph. Delhaye, *La théologie d'hier et d'aujourd'hui,* in *Rev. des Sciences Relig.,* April 1953, p. 122.

drama, the drama of our liberty between two loves, between two cities. He has described the deviations of our choice and the stratagems of grace with glowing, breathless, passionate psychological insight. It is on these grounds, because of this early incursion into the field of the *phenomenology* of human existence, rather than because of his philosophico-theological synthesis, which is rather uneven anyway, that St. Augustine remains the greatest moralist of all time.[7]

3. *The Appearance of Moralism*: *the Divorce of Dogma from Morality*

The actual directives

Moral theology, unless it is to run the risk of being unrealistic, should tackle the problems posed by personal and collective life. But it should do this by the light of faith as otherwise there is a danger that it may turn into opportunism, legalism and moralism, all of which are more concerned with imposing a moral behavior than with making such behavior spring from the heart. The thought of the Fathers of the Church in the great period is diametrically opposed to such a moralism, even when it descends to the most precise applications. Let anyone re-read the *Letters to Olympias* of St. John Chrysostom, those of St. Jerome— a feast for the mind in any case—and he will see that the lines of conduct, practical and adaptable, which they lay down are all wonderfully *linked to the truths of the faith,* and thereby animated by charity.

---

7. Cf. F. Van der Meer, *Saint Augustin pasteur d'âmes* (Paris 1955); T. Deman, *Le traitement scientifiques de la morale chrétienne selon saint Augustin* (Paris 1957).

St. Gregory the Great

In the case of a St. Gregory it might be considered that the Roman jurist triumphed over the spiritual writer. Apart altogether from an exegesis which is far too allegorical, his work on Job,[8] in his *Moralium Libri,* often seems to be that of a *rather narrow moralizer,* a pastor full of zeal but so eager to lecture his flock even down to mundane details that the broad highways of the new life in Christ no longer stand out. It is true that to make up for this he dwells very considerably on the eternal truths.

The "Penitentials"

Then came the barbarian invasions and soon there were scarcely any thinkers or theologians capable of sustaining the synthesis. Cut off from dogma, morality began to wither. The Irish monks, ascetics first and foremost and practical men, introduced into the West—or at all events spread widely—the exercise of private penance. The times were stern, the clergy scantily instructed. Yet confessors had to be formed. To meet the most urgent need there were composed the "Penitentials," *in other words, lists of faults with the scale of penances to be imposed.* The administration of the sacrament of penance having thus been reduced to the quasi-automatic application of these ready reckoners, moral teaching itself became entrenched in the mere interpreting of them .... By the tenth century there remained very little of the early and beautiful unity between faith and morality. The marriage was dissolved. There had been,

8. Gregory the Great, *Morales sur Job,* 1-11. See the Introduction by R. Gillet (Collection, "Sources chrétiennes," Paris 1950).

one might say, "a divorce due to faults on both sides." The one ray of hope which still lingered was that commentaries on the Scriptures remained in favor in the monasteries . . . .

II. THE SCHOLASTIC AGE: THE THEOLOGICAL SYNTHESES
(12th - 18th Centuries)

The trend of this second period may similarly be summarized as "from marriage to divorce."

1. *The New Marriage of Dogma and Morality*
(12th - 13th Centuries)

The ideal of the "Summas"

The twelfth Christian century is a wonderful century of renaissance. It should be awarded this title no less than the sixteenth century. In theology it is the springtime, a period of the bubbling over of ideas, of fermentation, of effervescence, of experiments of all kinds. The Scripture commentaries are complemented by "questions" and these in turn are soon built up into theological "summas." For us a "summa" means primarily an enormous bundle of folios, written in Latin, in a discouragingly technical language and according to the processes of a dialectic which often seems to have run wild. For the 13th century, the golden age of the "summas," they represented the *ideal of integral human scholarship*. Every young student as he progressed dreamed of turning his discoveries of truth into a synthesis which would embrace them in one broad sweep, his own unique vision of God. Morality could not fail to have its proper place therein.

St. Thomas Aquinas

The most successful of these "summas," though it was to remain uncompleted, is obviously that of St. Thomas. *One may search in vain through it for a morality existing as something separate.* The Second Part embraces a great many subjects which have a bearing on morality, but the author never saw morality as being something sufficient in itself. The way which brings man to God "at the speed of his acts" is not fixed by any teaching of the law, of human actions, of virtues and vices; it rests upon a doctrine of God (*First Part*) and continues through a doctrine of Christ and His Mystery (*Third Part*).[9]

Reason and Faith

The theological "summas" take up again the attempt of the Fathers to annex for the faith the treasures of philosophical thought. St. Thomas achieves in his "summa" a fairly adequate integration not only of the Platonic Stoicism found among the Fathers, but also of Aristotelean thought. Thereby was Aristotle duly baptized! But it is not Aristotle who dominates the theological "Summa," it is the Christian vision, inherited from the Bible and the faith, *of man created in the image of God.*[10] Practical applications, so

---

9. A. Plé, O.P., "Pour saint Thomas l'étude de la morale sur toute la Somme," *Supplément à la Vie Spirituelle*, 1956, pp. 6 and 12. Cf. M. Labourdette, O.P., *Revue thomiste*, 1950, p. 199.

10. Cf. in the *Summa Theologica*, the prologue of Part II, "Man being made in the image of God ...." etc.

overwhelming among certain authors, produce here the multiple "Questions" but without dominating the development of the thought, without prejudice to its movement and to its profound unity. The theological line of thought remains indissolubly speculative and practical.

2. *Unity between Faith and Morality in a new compromise* (14 - 18th centuries)

The "Summas of the confessors"

The unity so happily effected in the theological "Summas" of the great era very quickly deteriorated. The Lateran Council (1215) had just made Easter confession obligatory. The canonist movement of the *Decretals* reorganized penitential discipline. The "summas for confessors," facilitating the questioning of penitents by *lists, often alphabetical, of sins,* now took on the force of the old "penitentials." They were tremendously useful tools, less bulky, indeed, than the "summas" of theology, but ones which *led directly to a purely negative and minimalist teaching.* For on the one hand there was the confessor who needed to know first and foremost all that should not be done, and on the other the penitent who, because of his natural propensity, wanted to know the minimum that had to be fulfilled under pain of sin.

The theological "summas" continued to be taught in the universities. They were to attain their apogee in *monumental works* and with great éclat like that of the *Carmelites of Salamanca.* But who as yet had the leisure to attend the university? The majority of priests pursued only the courses in the diocesan school, where St. Thomas was scarcely known at all. Since the law of the majority

54

operated in favor of the "summas for confessors," the grave risk was run of reducing moral theology to these latter, which were handed around without any protection from the proliferation of casuistry.

The "Institutiones Morales"

Hope stirred in the 16th and 17th centuries. In a positive effort at genuine reform the Jesuits felt the need to interpose between the huge "summas" of theology for the universities and the "practical summas" for confessors something which held a little of both, *a type of work which would be at once very practical and yet reasonably solid from the speculative point of view*. The Council of Trent had in fact adopted a most exacting attitude in respect to the administration of the sacrament of penance. In particular it had demanded that one should declare one's sins in a precise way, giving the category into which they fell, their particular nature, their number—all so so many items to be explained to the confessors. It was at this exact moment in history that there came into being those books destined to serve successfully for three centuries, the "Institutiones Morales." Going much further than the practical recipes for confession, the "Institutiones Morales" aimed to inculcate those elements essential to a true moral science by giving an outline of the principles and the great theses of morality. Despite this laudable aim they did not restore the unity of dogma and morality, for they are preoccupied primarily with sorting sins into legal categories rather than inspired by a living theology. We are all familiar with this class of writing—the treatises on moral theology officially in use in the majority of seminaries today are still these "Institutiones Morales" brought up to date. In these books there is very little mention of God, of Christ, of the Church and of the situation of man in the Mystery of faith. The morality in them is still minimalist, centered upon the sin to be avoided. Christian perfection, relegated as a subject in itself to the end of the book, or regarded as a matter for a spiritual manual, is made to appear in fact as something reserved for eccentrics. Yet in spite of systematization and careful arrangement these "Institutiones Morales" lack unity and Christian synthesis, and one seeks in vain for the spirit animating the entire sequence of chapters, unless it be the wholly negative one of avoidance of sin.

3. *St. Alphonsus Liguori* (✝ 1787)

A man of his time, the model of the moralists, St. Alphonsus, while drawing up his own work in the style of the "Institutiones Morales," conceived it primarily in his capacity as *pastor of souls and not as a professor.* It broke his apostolic heart to see theologians spending their time in rival scholastic disputes (rigorists and laxists; probabilists and probabiliorists), while the faithful were left exposed to the assaults of the eighteenth century. It was through pastoral charity that he committed himself to the onerous undertaking of selecting and piecing together, from the rubbish heap of moral opinions current in his day, *a sure code of moral behavior,* and of putting an end to the disputes by a doctrine of *just balance between law and liberty.* One may say that in this he succeeded and that as a result of his work these great quarrels will never again be of more than minor interest.

Of his spiritual writing (*The Practice of Love towards Jesus Christ, The Great Means of Prayer,* etc.) which was inspired by an ardent love of Christ, and was extremely popular, one might say that by its strange dualism it either emphasizes the divorce between morality and faith or, alternatively, that it promises an inevitable reintegration of them.

III. THE MODERN EPOCH: IN QUEST OF A NEW SYNTHESIS

Dogma and morality, separated, seek one another for they cannot live without each other. But who will be the architect of their reconciliation?

1. *Two tendencies towards a renewal since the last century*

The Neo-scholastic Movement

Returning to the lines of direction enunciated by St. Alphonsus, Christian moralists of the 19th century saw in them the way of prudence and of wisdom for the Church. Under the influence of renewed contact with the Middle Ages, however, they sought to complement this practical morality and its pastoral directives with a *theoretical* morality, *inspired in particular by St. Thomas,* but they merely succeeded in maintaining at high level the genre of the "Institutiones Morales."

The Theological School of Tübingen

In our view the attempt by the Tübingen school to evolve a new synthesis is more interesting. French workers in this field are especially familiar with the work of its great dogmatists and, in particular, that of J. A. Möhler who, in his theological concept of the Church, goes back to the thought of the Fathers. Now this revival in the field of dogma set in motion a revival in that of moral theology, thus confirming the law which says that they go hand in hand.

Among those who promoted this revival mention must be made of J. M. Sailer and J. B. Hirscher who have also played their part in developing modern catechesis. They are two of the most discussed men of their time, and rightly so, even if one of the points of discussion is their remarkable failure to discern the useless elements in the philosophical thought of that epoch. Nevertheless they restored the meaning of Christian morality which does not consist in a list of sins to be avoided or a minimum obligation to be fulfilled but is for all men *a life of striving for perfection through the imitation of Christ in the Kingdom of God.*

2. *The Current Trend*

French Thomism, resting upon solid, erudite research,[11] entered the lists around the year 1950 with l'*Initiation Théologique,* the third volume of which, showing here and there the influence of the biblical renewal, is entitled "Moral Theology."

A theologian and exegetist from Bonn, F. Tillmann, has, since the beginning of 1932, completed a manual of Catholic moral teaching (in seven volumes) around the central theme of the imitation of Jesus Christ. Inspired by the efforts of the Tübingen school he *grafted morality once more upon the Bible and the Fathers,* and not upon the Law, so that

----

11. And, it must be said, on innumerable practical studies, especially of social or family morality.

58

the sap rising in it might be authentically Christian. The collaboration of T. Steinbüchel and T. Muncker brought to this work the complement of a philosophic thought at once lucid and daring.

It is in the wake of all this that Fr. Bernard Häring, a Redemptorist of the province of Munich, published in 1954 a volume of 1,500 pages called *The Law of Christ: Moral Theology for Priests and Laity*. He wished, while being attentive to the appeals and needs of his era, to respond to them in the spirit of the loftiest demands of the Evangelical law. The result has been *a morality of the Spirit of Christ in which everything seems really governed by charity*. Despite its success—100,000 copies in German and translation, since the first of these appeared in 1962 have been sold—it is an incomplete work. It is a profoundly spiritual work "in which daring," as Mgr. Garrone says in his preface to the French edition, "really only aims at perfect fidelity, and novelty only the reward of a more instant call to Tradition."

In the spirit of *The Law of Christ*, in the translation—adaptation of which we collaborated, we shall expound the great themes and essential pronouncements of a Christian morality. No one will then be surprised to find that our study of each of these has its roots in a reflection upon a particular dogma. That makes sense for anyone who has learnt the paramount lesson taught by the vicissitudes of moral theology down the ages.

All that remains before embarking on this analysis is to justify our division of it which is based upon the actual mysteries of Christ.

CHAPTER THREE

THE LAW OF CHRIST IN HIS MYSTERIES

If it be true that the law for the Christian is wholly the law of Christ how can anyone claim to expound its principles in detail without revealing the Mystery of the life of Christ? That Mystery and that life are one. Why not, then, abide by the evangelical simplicity of the dictum "follow Christ," "imitate Christ?" Why not adopt the Pauline epigram: "I live, now not I, but Christ liveth in me," and leave it at that?

Nothing in fact is simpler than life, in the sense that nothing has more "oneness." But nothing is richer, either, than its synthesis, especially as one ascends the scale in the hierarchy of beings. The increasing complexity of living beings (the "parameter of complexity and of cephalization" as Teilhard de Chardin says!) is the very condition of their stronger oneness. Analogically the supernatural life takes on the force of this law. It is marvelously "one" yet incomparably rich. The same Paul who brings back everything to Christ, knows that *in His mystery "are hid all the treasures of wisdom and of knowledge"* (Coloss. II, 3). "Christ liveth in me," but it is still essential to grow in the knowledge of this miracle of love which, in very truth, "surpasseth all knowledge" (Eph. III, 19). "And this I pray, that your charity may more and more abound in knowledge and in all understanding: that you may approve the better things" (Phil. I, 9, 10).

This *mystery* of Christ of which Paul so unwearingly writes in his letters from prison ("As you reading, understand my knowledge in the mystery of Christ" Eph. III, 4)—this mystery God has unfolded *in the mysteries* which the Liturgy, in conjunction with the sacraments, brings to life for us every year. In order to establish the unity of the fundamental principles of Christian morality by relating all of them to Christ, but without thereby lapsing into an impoverishing simplification, it is obvious that one must refer to these mysteries.

We shall consider successively the great mysteries of *Easter,* (I) *Pentecost,* (II) and the *Parousia* liturgically: *Christmas* or the *Epiphany,* feasts of the Manifestation of the Lord, directed towards the present and the future quite as much as towards the past (III).

Is not the Christian the "man of Easter and Pentecost" as Père Congar says?[1] While Paul also defines him as one who lives "looking for the blessed hope and coming of the glory of the great God and our Savior Jesus Christ" (Titus II, 13).

Not only does the unique Mystery of Christ open out in these three mysteries, but His light, as though through a triple prism, shines through them, breaking up into separate rays for us. It is from these mysteries that we shall take all the necessary conditions of the *New Law* which we shall examine one by one. We shall be able to relate the latter continuously to their triple source; their purpose will merely be to set out the requirements for us to identify them with the mysteries of Christ. Our law is *Christ in His mysteries.*

▬▬▬▬▬▬▬▬▬▬▬▬▬▬▬

1. *Si vous êtes mes témoins,* Paris 1959, pp. 10, 35, etc.

I. THE LAW OF CHRIST AND THE MYSTERY OF EASTER

The paschal law and the law of the covenant

The majority of manuals of moral theology begin—with some reason, but not without some risk—with a treatise on the attainment of heavenly bliss. This is a reasonable beginning since the way a person acts is obviously governed by what he wants to attain, but it is not without risk because this is not a matter of halting at an ideal of self-perfection, of happiness to be found in the conquest of self, since we are invited to turn away from ourselves and towards God, as to our *supernatural* end, in Jesus Christ. Let us say that generally speaking anyhow, where these treatises have a philosophical basis, the emphasis is not on Jesus Christ.

1. *The Christian End of Man*

Breaking, like Fr. Häring,[2] with this tradition—"which is more honored in the breach than the observance," as Hamlet says[3]—Fr. J. Fuchs in his recent *General Moral Theology* starts right away with a *Christian* conception of human life—man, in accordance with God's plan, finds his end in the divine relationship by *assimilation in Christ*, and particularly in the Christ of the Resurrection. This fact from Revelation should serve as the keystone of our morality[4] and one can but rejoice at this and be surprised at the reserve it arouses here and there.

---

2. Cf. *La loi du Christ*, I. 5th edition, pp. 63-66.

3. "...it is a custom more honour'd in the breach than the observance" (Hamlet, Act I, sc. 4).

4. Cf. J. Fuchs, S.J., *Theologica moralis generalis*, Pars prima, Rome 1960, pp. 21 et seq.: *Conceptio christiana vitae humanae.*

This, in fact, is the fundamental principle of St. Paul's morality—Christ, and very precisely, the Christ of Easter, *Christ dead and risen again.* And there is no necessity to contrast the historical Christ with the Christ of glory, as if the whole life of Christ did not lead towards that glory, as if it were not entirely polarized by that glory—that glory of the Only Son which was indicated at His birth and on the occasion of His Baptism, which burst forth at the Transfiguration and established itself as stronger than death on Easter morning. Paul can say quite as correctly that he is "crucified with Christ" (Rom. VI, 6; cf. Gal. II, 19) and that he "catches the glory of the Lord as in a mirror" (II Cor. III, 18). The Incarnation in flesh which can feel and suffer, the Passion, Death and Resurrection form but one Mystery, that of the "Passage" of the humanity of Christ to His Father. And this mystery is the authoritative standard of our morality.[5]

The risen Christ is in fact our perfect model, "the new man who according to God is created in justice and holiness of truth" (Eph. IV, 24). He is more than our model; He is the very *principle* of what makes us new. "If then any be in Christ a new creature, the old things are passed away, behold all things are made new" (II Cor. V, 17). Lead a

----

5. Fr. Congar speaks with good reason of a "program of the Christian life, of the Christian ethic, as a *paschal* program," (*Si vous êtes mes témoins,* p. 26).

Fr. Durrwell, in his great work, *La Résurrection mystère de salut,* 3rd edition, revised and augmented, Ed. Mappus, Paris, 1955, says: "The risen Christ is the principle of Christian morality.... The new morality is governed by the paschal mystery; it is a *law of death and of resurrection*" (pp. 286-287).

new life, then, you whom baptism has plunged into the Death and the Resurrection of the Lord (cf. Rom. VI, 4), a life of justice and of holiness, a life of paschal incorruption, a life which fully reflects the divine glory. "So do you also reckon that you are *dead* to sin, but *alive* unto God, in Christ Jesus our Lord" (Rom. VI, 11). "Therefore, if you be risen with Christ, seek the things that are above" (Coloss. III, 1). If a major feast for Christian morality is sought there can be no other.

Risen from the dead, become what you are!

Undoubtedly the elliptical precept of Pindar, "Become what you are," has a value for us, too. "We must live our baptismal consecration and become what we are," writes Fr. Durrwell.[6] And Feuillet writes:

"Having been dead and risen again with Christ at baptism, we still have to become more every day what we are; we have to die and to rise again daily, to learn to know Christ ever better, and the transforming virtue of His resurrection, as says the Epistle to the Philippians (III, 10), through communion with His sufferings and assimilation into His death."[7]

"You have put on Christ" (Gal. III, 27); "Put ye on the Lord Jesus Christ" (Rom. XIII, 14). "Purge out the old leaven, that you may be a new paste, as you are *unleavened*" (I Cor. V, 7). "Our old man is crucified" (Rom. VI, 6); "Put off the old man ... and be renewed" (Eph. IV, 22,

---

6. F. X. Durrwell, *op. cit.*, p. 288.

7. A. Feuillet: *La Résurrection des chrétiens d'après saint Paul*, in the *Nouvelle Revue théologique*, 1957, pp. 343-344.

23). "God ... hath raised us up together in Christ and made us sit together in the heavenly places" (Eph. II, 4-6); "... let us bear also the image of the heavenly" (I Cor. XV, 49). We need only to replace these quotations in their context to realize that Paul is, of course, speaking about the moral life, or rather that he does not separate the suffering and the resurrection of the flesh from the spiritualization of our being which commences at baptism; "in the thought of the Apostle *the two points of view are united.*"[8] Our morality is a *baptismal* morality and therefore *paschal,* and it involves us, through the Cross, in an incorruption of morals, which is in turn the pledge and prelude to the incorruption of the flesh in the final resurrection.

2. *Paschal Morality, The Morality of the Covenant*

There has not been sufficient reflection upon the *Trinitarian* import of the *Paschal* mystery.[9] That glory which God communicated to Christ in His Resurrection is His eternal glory ("the glory which I had, before the world was, with thee," John XVII, 5), that is to say, His power, His strength, His own Being, that unique Nature which the Father communicated to His Son in engendering Him, and the brilliance of which the Son did not seek to keep in His Incarnation. "Who being in the form of God" (Phil. II, 6)

8. A. Feuillet: *art. cit.,* p. 352.

9. This point seems to us to be of capital importance. Meditating, in another context on the *Encounter with the other* (a Trinitarian subject) and on the *Paschal mystery,* one of us wrote: "This will constitute a leap forward for the theological synthesis which will show their *convergence*" (*Masses Ouvrières,* Oct. 1960, No. 4, p. 19). We are here trying to make an approach of this kind.

—"born in this glory" as Bossuet puts it—"empties himself ... becoming obedient unto death, even to the death of the cross" (Phil. II, 7-8). That is why God exalted Him and restored to Him *His filial glory even in His body.* He has, as it were, reengendered Him, giving to Him again in a new way and in a new corporal reality, "the name which is above all names" (Phil. II, 9).

Paschal glory, filial glory

It is worth noting how the verse of Psalm II which we sing at Christmas to greet the birth of Christ, "The Lord hath said to me: Thou art my son; this day have I begotten thee," is applied by Scripture to the Resurrection:

"... The promise which was made to our fathers, this same God hath fulfilled to our children raising up Jesus, as in the second psalm also is written: *Thou art my Son, this day have I begotten thee*" (Acts XIII, 33). See, too, in their context of Paschal glorification, the quotations from Hebrews I, 5 and V, 5. Paul is equally explicit: "Who was predestined the Son of God in power, according to the spirit of sanctification by the resurrection of our Lord Jesus Christ from the dead" (Rom. I, 4).

Filial glory, the glory of the Word

Now, how did God engender His Son? From all eternity, *by uttering the word* He begot Him as His Word, as His eternal Yes, the perfect Response who called Him "Father," and by communicating to Him, at that same instant, His glory. The earthly Adam had said "No" to God. He had said, "I will not serve." The heavenly Adam obeyed. "In him all is affirmed with certainty" (II Cor. I, 19). He is the Amen (Apoc. III, 14). Hence His glory. This glory of the Resurrertion is but the showing forth in His flesh of the Yes of His Passion. Each in its turn is in the direct line of the generation of the Word, of the eternal Yes. "Yea, Father: for so hath it seemed good in thy sight" (Matt. XI, 26). "... I do always the things that please him" (John VIII, 29). I am always whatever He wills! "My Father, ... thy will be done" (Matt. XXVI, 42). "... glorify thou me, O Father" (John XVII, 5). Jesus allows Himself to be called by the Father.

Such is our model, such our inner strength, the risen Christ, the perfect response to the Father. It is here that a treatise on the end and purpose of life should be able to achieve its full profundity. What is the meaning of our being? In whose image have we been created? We have been created in the image of the Son, in the image of the Word, capable, therefore, of saying Yes to God, and through this Yes, capable of being begotten by the Father, capable of having a share in His glory if He makes His call clear to us. Now, "he also predestined (us) to be made conformable to the image of his Son" (Rom. VIII, 29). In the baptismal union with Jesus dead and risen again we receive "the spirit of *adoption* of sons, whereby we cry Abba (Father)" (Rom. VIII, 15). "For you are the *children of God by faith* in Christ Jesus. For as many of you as have been baptized in Christ, have put on Christ" (Gal. III, 26-27). The supernatural end assumes the natural end and carries it out. We are naturally capable of responding to God, and we are supernaturally "called" by Him, and "justified" and "glorified" (cf. Rom. VIII, 30). All this is in Christ: "... for it is through him that we say our 'Amen' to the glory of God" (II Cor. I, 20), and it is through Him that we

shall enter therefore into that glory. To be united with
Christ is to answer Yes to God.

This is the morality of Easter, the morality of the filial
response to God, since, in assimilation with the risen Christ,
our response fuses with that of the Word. Thus Easter
introduces us to the leading idea of Christian morality,
namely, that it is a dialogical morality, or, if you like, a
law of the covenant.

The Law of Christ is the *Paschal law and the law of the
covenant.* The mystery is the mystery of baptism to Christ,
the sacrament of *faith.* This says everything, for the glory
to which we are baptized is Trinitarian, which implies the
gift of the Holy Spirit who brings with Him *freedom* and
charity.

II. THE NEW LAW AND THE MYSTERY
OF PENTECOST

*The Law of the Spirit, the Law of the Church
and the Law of Charity*

Whether or not the starting point for morality consists
in a treatise on the attainment of heavenly bliss, it is certainly common to assign the quality of obligation to morality
as the norm. "You must; you are bound; that is what the
Law says." In revenge we should adopt as our golden rule
the extremely unevangelical maxim: *True charity begins at
home!*

Paul himself never tires of telling us: In Christ you are
free; set free from the Law and its constraints. "You have
been called unto *liberty*" (Gal. V, 13). "For *the end of the
law* is Christ" (Rom. X, 4). With what vigor he denounces

the "false brethren... who came in privately to spy our *liberty* which we have in Christ Jesus, that they might bring us into servitude" (Gal. II, 4). On the other hand, he closely unites this liberty with *charity towards others* (Gal. V, 13-14). How do these fit in with one another? The key to this contradiction must be sought in the *Holy Spirit*, the soul of the Church, the Spirit of both liberty and love.

1. *The Morality of Pentecost: the Morality of the Spirit of Freedom*

Is not Christ's victory over death on Easter morning the confirmation of a *perfect freedom?* He is no longer subject in any way to the elements of this world (Gal. IV, 3; cf. Coloss. II, 20-22). In Him "we are the slaves of guilt no longer" (Rom. VI, 6). Our Easter is to us our Exodus, our *deliverance* from Egypt, as we sing of it during Easter Night.

This deliverance, obtained at Easter, is blazoned forth at Pentecost. With predilection Paul relates the freedom of the Christian to the gift of the Holy Spirit, "the Spirit (which) breatheth where he will" (John III, 8). "...where the Spirit of the Lord is, there is liberty" (II Cor. III, 17). The texts are numberless. They speak always, of course, of the Paschal mystery of which Pentecost—the fiftieth day— is but the fulfillment (*cum complerentur dies Pentecostes*). The Holy Spirit comes to give explicit expression, in us, to the triumph of Christ.[10]

----

10. St. Augustine: "Note here how the solemnity of Easter has reached its conclusion without losing anything of its wonder. Easter has been the commencement of grace, Pentecost is its crown." Sermon 43, quoted by Père Congar, *La Pentecôte, Chartres*, 1956, p. 31. He himself frequently repeats: "Pentecost is the fulfillment of Easter."

This Spirit who, in sudden fiery exhalation, gave visible testimony of His presence, and conferred upon the fearful Apostles their freedom to move out and to speak openly—our *confirmation* should procure for us the same courage—is the Spirit of the *Resurrection*. He who filled Christ to make of Him, even in His own body, a "quickening Spirit" (I Cor. XV, 45; cf. Coloss. II, 9). Christ already gave His Apostles the first fruits of Him on the evening of Easter Day (John XX, 22). This spirit loosens all bonds.

Why? First of all because He is a filial Spirit, for was not Christ "predestined the *Son of God . . . according to the spirit of sanctification* (Rom. I, 4)? "For whosoever are led by the Spirit of God, they are the sons of God" (Rom. VIII, 14). That is what explains our freedom—it is a filial freedom (Rom. VIII, 21). For the sons of the Master are free. We were slaves, but "God sent his Son . . . to redeem them who were under the law: that we might receive the adoption of sons. And because you are sons, God hath sent the Spirit of his Son into your hearts, crying: Abba, Father. Therefore now he is not a servant, but a son . . ." (Gal. IV, 4-7). "For you have not received the spirit of bondage . . . you have received the spirit of adoption of sons, whereby we cry: Abba (Father)" (Rom. VIII, 15).

Naturally this freedom is not synonymous with anarchy. "Make not liberty an occasion to the flesh" (Gal. V, 13). But what is there in common between the Spirit and the flesh? "I say then, walk in the spirit, and you shall not fulfill the lusts of the flesh" (Gal. V, 16). And here a strange paradox comes into action: between the flesh and the spirit there is opposition, "for these are contrary one to another so that you do not the things that you would. But if you are led by the spirit, you are not under the law" (Gal. V, 17-18). So, "stand fast, and be not held again under the yoke of bondage" (Gal. V, 1). One should never weary of reading and re-reading these statements and of meditating on their implications. We must correct sensuality even in our bodies if we want to be able to do what we wish.

Inner liberty

No one has dealt better with this dialectic, in pages which these aforesaid manuals have unfortunately allowed to remain very much in obscurity, than St. Thomas Aquinas:

"The will, being of its nature directed to what is truly good, when a man under the influence of a passion, of a vice or of an evil disposition, turns away from what is truly good, such a man, *if one consider the essential direction* of the will, acts as a slave, since he now allows himself to go against that direction through the pressure of some foreign principle. But if one consider the action of the will *as being actually inclined towards an apparent good,* then he acts freely when he follows his passion or his corrupt disposition, and he acts as a slave if, his will still remained turned in the same way, he abstains from what he wants to do through fear of the law established against this.

"But in fact the Spirit of God inclines the will, through love, towards the true good, through love He arranges that the will actually leans wholly towards that which is indeed in keeping with its own deepest desire. Therefore He removes at the same time both forms of slavery: the slavery in which, the serf of passion and of sin, man acts against the natural direction of his will; and the slavery in which, the serf of the law and not its friend, he acts according to the law against the motion of his will. *Where is the*

72

Spirit of the Lord, says the Apostle Paul, *there is liberty;* and, *If you are led by the Spirit you are not under the law.*"[11]

This is not to say, however, that we are absolutely without law: "...I was not without the law of God, but was in the law of Christ" (I Cor. IX, 21). But there is a "law of liberty" (James II, 12), "the law of the spirit of life, in Christ Jesus, hath delivered me from the law of sin and of death" (Rom. VIII, 2). *Our standard is Christ, by virtue of the Spirit of Christ,* the very opposite of an impersonal obligation. "It should be vigorously repeated that the children of God no longer live under a law, within a regime, within a system of salvation whose principle is a law. Here indeed stands the innovation of the New Covenant—the promotion to liberty."[12]

2. *The Morality of Pentecost: The Morality of the Ecclesial Spirit*

Fine words, it may be said. But what about proving the necessity to *obey* God's law even when it is painful to us? After all, why should I not call whatever suits me the law of the Spirit? I would be going against my conscience. I could train that! It is here that reference to the Church-Body of Christ is indispensable. No one can claim to have the Spirit of Christ who evades His Body.

The mystery of Pentecost can instill it into us better than any reasoning—the appearance of the Church was strictly contemporaneous with the gift of the Spirit, or rather one could go so far as to say that the gift of the Spirit was the birth of the Church, because this Spirit is the

---

11. *Summa contra Gentiles:* IV, 22.
12. Spicq: *Charité et liberté selon le Nouveau Testament,* Paris 1961, p. 72. (Alba House 1965)

Spirit of love. While He distributes His gifts "to everyone according as he will" (I Cor. XII, 11), it is always the same Spirit in the service of the same Body. There is no other, and no one can lay any claim to arrogate Him to himself, separately from all the rest: "For *in one Spirit* were we all baptized *into one body*" (I Cor. XII, 13). The Spirit who leads each according to His wish does so only within the Church, and cannot act in contradiction to "the Apostles and ancients, with the whole church" (Acts XV, 22) when they say, "it hath seemed good to the Holy Ghost and to us" (Acts XV, 28). It is indeed the Spirit of truth who sets us free (cf. John VIII, 32 and XVI, 13), but the Church is His temple, "the pillar and the ground of truth" (I Tim. III, 15). Besides, is it not in the Church that we are children of God, and therefore free?

The Church is all the more surely the framework of our freedom in that she is the center of our *charity* and that charity governs freedom.

3. The Morality of Pentecost: The Morality of the Spirit of Love

The *freedom* of the Spirit is accorded to us only in company with the *charity* which He diffuses in our hearts. "It is the love of charity which makes the freedom of the sons," says St. Thomas.[13] Moved by this love which God bears me, I in my turn love both Christ and my brethren because I love the Father. And because this love corresponds to something which wells up in my own nature, I find my freedom in this love of *others*. Why? Because I am made in the image of God for this dialogue of love.

---

13. IIa-IIae, q. 184, a. 4, ad. 1.

74

My freedom through love of others

This is not, then, a simple question of making the law inwardly compelling, the law which has now become the principle of *my* action.   Faith is in me, but it makes me adhere to Christ; hope is in me but it makes me find my support in Christ; charity is in me but it hands me over to Christ, and when Christ has left the earth, the *role of His Spirit of love is precisely to make me recognize Him in my brethren.* It is for that reason that it was a good thing for Christ to depart, so that I might not seek Him here or there, but in all men.   That is also why the sacrament of His love, the Eucharist, is celebrated in all places where many are gathered in His name in order to signify His presence effectively "until he come" (I Cor. XI, 26).

I do not call upon the Spirit Himself in order to possess Him, but to be possessed by Him who brings me back to the Father and to the Son.   He is not within me to teach me charity towards myself; He is in me who said "Father" and who makes me know my brethren in Jesus Christ.   This is charity, *for me,* and the supreme fulfillment of my being; whoever loses self finds this.   Let us listen to St. Paul: "For you, brethren, have been called unto liberty: only make not liberty an occasion to the flesh, but by *charity* of the spirit serve one another.   For all the law is fulfilled in one word: *Thou shalt love thy neighbor as thyself"* (Gal. V, 13-14).

The truth of our life

We are far from the convenient maxim "True charity begins . . . ."   When will we stop slanting texts which are equally clear?   Paul did not say, "Love yourselves in order to fulfill the law of charity;" he said, "Love others."   But for that, it may be said, I must restrain myself. Very well, but the whole question is to know if I should restrain myself through love for me, or through love of God and of others. To give one's life for those whom one loves is the example set by Christ, and the inspiration of His Spirit. There is nothing more restrictive of self than this forgetfulness of self. Is it *for himself* that Paul is suffering when he says, "Always bearing about in our body the mortification of Jesus, that the life also of Jesus may be made manifest in our bodies" (II Cor. IV, 10)? He answers that himself. "I now rejoice in my sufferings *for you*, and fill up those things that are wanting of the sufferings of Christ in my flesh, for his body, which is the church" (Coloss. I, 24).

The Spirit of Christ dedicates us to God in Jesus Christ and we dedicate ourselves to others as to the "sacraments of Christ." The whole meaning of our lives should be to see, and to make visible in each of our brethren, the Well-Beloved Son in whom the Father was well pleased. It is in that charity that we find the truth of our lives and it is this truth which makes us free. This is what at our best we would desire.

The law of Christ is the law of filial freedom, promulgated as it were at Pentecost with the birth of the Church, the *law of the Spirit* and the *law of the Church*—in short, the *law of charity*.

III. THE LAW OF CHRIST AND THE MYSTERY OF THE PAROUSIA

The law of growth through earthly mediations

A code of rights and duties properly drawn up, isolated if possible in the religious domain, the methodical observance of which will at least merit an honorable place in a heavenly paradise—this, unfortunately, is the ideal of a great many Christian consciences! For them the dogma of the Resurrection is just a symbol of the immortality of the soul. Why should religion involve itself in our actions during every day we spend in this world, the world of mortal bodies, since the paradise to which it leads is not of this world, and *has nothing to do with material affairs?* Day to day morality is a matter of commonly observed conventions, and mainly one of politeness. Appearances must be properly kept up in a world where the unwritten law is still "every man for himself," in a jungle in which one must cope with sordid necessities. It would be ridiculous to bring God into this mundane record. There is, in fact, no manual of moral theology which would ratify this separation, but more than one unwittingly encourages it by proffering nothing better than a *static* morality, a reflection of natural prudence and commonsense.

1. *The Lord Will Come Again*

Oh, that the mystery of the Parousia—the supreme revelation of the mystery of Easter and perfect accomplishment of Pentecost—might condemn such unreality! No, it is not true that we anticipate at the end of this life the simple immortality of the individual soul, the happiness of my soul united with God. We anticipate something quite different. We await *Someone,* the risen Lord Himself, who will come again to this world to transform our bodies from wretchedness into the body of his glory (Phil. III, 21) in accordance with the way in which we directed our lives every day at the heart of this changing world. If Pentecost clearly indicates the road which Easter lays open to us, if the Holy Spirit shows us that this new life is freedom and charity, freedom through charity, the Parousia teaches us

77

that this charity must be expressed here on earth in the world of the body and must increase unto the return of the Lord, "unto a perfect man, unto the measure of the age of the fulness of Christ" of which St. Paul speaks (Eph. IV, 13). It preserves us from all angelism and from all desire to avoid the carnal world.

We sing of it in the Credo: *descendit de coelis*. Cajetan may well frown at the metaphor of the God who descends, and emphasize that it is rather a matter of the humanity which ascends, assumed by God. It remains true that the Son of God has come among His own in flesh and bone. This first coming of Christ (Coming=Parousia) which we celebrate in the cycle of Christmas and the Epiphany, is to us the guarantee of His second coming: [14] *Et iterum venturus est*. He will come again. *Quaemadmodum vidistis eum euntem in coelum*. You have seen Him go. He will return in the same way. Do not say, His name will be celebrated, His merits will be extolled, men will confess His glory.... That is not enough. He will come again in person. He will manifest Himself (Manifestation=Epiphany).

2. *Heaven*

What He will do when He comes concerns not only our souls but our bodies, our whole being: "...but ourselves also, who have the first fruits of the Spirit, even we ourselves groan within ourselves, waiting for the...redemption of our body. For we are saved by hope" (Rom.

▪▪▪▪▪▪▪▪▪▪▪▪▪▪▪

14. Dom Claude Jean-Nesmy published a trilogy: *Spiritualité pascale, Spiritualité de la Pentecôte, Spiritualité de Noël*. He has explained very well the reason for making this latter volume the third of the trilogy—the Mystery of Advent is always before us.

VIII, 23, 24). The whole of Creation will participate in this new birth. "For the expectation of the creature waiteth for the revelation of the sons of God . . . . That the creature also itself shall be delivered from the servitude of corruption, into the liberty of the children of God" (Rom. VIII, 19-21). If Paul sees us being taken up "in the clouds to meet Christ" (I Thess. IV, 17), it is not in order to fly from this world, which is for ever subject to Christ (Heb. II, 8), but as the inhabitants hereafter of "new heavens" and "a new earth" (II Pet. III, 13).

So, by a supreme outpouring of His Spirit—an ultimate Pentecost—Christ will crown our freedom in charity and, submerged in the divine glory, we shall be borne away with our whole being and the world to which it belongs into the unending exchange of Trinitarian relations. And for that to come to pass we shall have no need to leave this world where God is. (It is the Church which descends in the wake of Christ, and certainly, first of all, of the Blessed Virgin. Apoc. XXI, 1-4). Then it will be apparent that God is with us and that we are in Him for ever.

3. *On Earth*

Such is our expectation. Why then should anyone be surprised that it does not mean living at the peak of the spirit only, but of exercising our freedom and our charity through *matter* itself, subject as it is to change and development; of accepting, of seeking its *mediation* as much for our communion with God—and note here how the *liturgy* is completely involved in signs which are apparent to the senses—as for our communion with our neighbor. Note, in regard to the latter, that the primary care of *service inspired by charity* is to insure for others, in the domain of material advantages, the benefit of perfect justice in an atmosphere of love free from arguments about mine and thine.

These two mediations are intertwined. For the Eucharist, the manna of our journey to eternity, the sacrament through which we untiringly announce the death of the Lord "until he come" (I Cor. XI, 26), refers us every day to the most humble brotherly charity, that which consists in feeding others with everything for which they hunger here below, so that, through the generosity of the sons of God, they may find in the satisfaction of their immediate needs a pledge of hope. When the Lord returns all the stakes will have been lost or won, for we shall already have accepted or repudiated Him. But we are so sluggish in our belief that even we, as well forewarned as we are, will keep on asking: "Lord, ... when did we see thee a stranger, and took thee in?" (Matt. XXV, 37, 38). The mystery of the Parousia includes the fact that the Lord anticipates His return. The most insignificant of suffering humanity suffices for Him to give us a sign; the least of His little ones affords us the opportunity to recognize Him.

4. *Newness and Growth*

Liturgy and the acceptance of others are things which cannot be compressed into a list of hard and fast duties to form a tight and static morality. *Charity which involves itself with the material world cannot help but develop along with it.* It must take cognizance of the new demands arising out of the changing conditions which the ingenuity of men creates in our world. However much our selfish interests may oppose this movement, and however much they may pervert it ("But yet the Son of Man, when He cometh, shall He find, think you, faith on earth?" (Luke XVIII, 8), we know that this movement is always evolving towards Christ under the guidance of the Spirit.

Of prayer

The liturgy, and in its train, private prayer, are living things. They have changed in the course of the centuries. (One has but to examine the long history of the Mass, or that of Penance, or again, that of public prayer to see this). They will change again. This will come to pass, if we are faithful to the Spirit, only in the form of an increased expression of our free filial love, *through the signs best adapted to every epoch;* they will be more eloquent, more authentic, dedicating us all together ever more effectively to the glory of "Him who is,—and who was,—and who is to come" (Apoc. I, 8). And, of course, they will need to be extended with the missionary Church throughout the whole earth.

And of charity

Charity in this life will never cease to bombard us with its appeals, appeals which are always the same and yet always new because society is always changing. The march of civilization is creating increasing possibilities among us of intercommunication which react upon all our obligations. My neighbor is no longer my next-door neighbor; rather, he who suffers at the remotest end of the earth is in the process of becoming my next-door neighbor (the time is at hand when all the capitals of the world will be no more than an hour's distance apart and here and now we have TV, radio, etc.). The growth is not only extensive, but also intensive. In the name of charity the *threefold unification* achieved, as St. Paul tells us in Christ, must become ever truer: what must be continuously diminished is, not the enriching diversity but the inequalities between male and female, between Barbarian and Greek, poor countries and rich countries, bond and free, laborers and employers. We are still very far wide of the mark, but we do know that in Christ it is in this sense that history evolves; it is in this sense that we must move with it towards the Parousia.

Until the appointed time

When will this break upon the world? Undoubtedly when suitable conditions shall have prepared the way for it. If Christ formerly waited upon Scripture to come among His own, for what will He wait in the matter of His second coming? Perhaps until science has learnt to retard physical death indefinitely, in order that He may bind up our broken hearts by bringing back all those already dead and gathering us all together into a much better life? We do not know. But we are able to think that in working for the progress of the world *in the direction of charity* we are hastening the appointed time.[15]

What holds good for what happens during the course of the slow drift of the centuries holds good now for *every one of our lives.* Each one of us must, conformably with the Spirit, grow towards the encounter with the Lord, accepting the fact that we must progressively discern ever more clearly the appeals of Christ; must live the Sacrifice of the Mass more keenly, must respond ever more effectively

▄▄▄▄▄▄▄▄▄▄▄▄▄▄▄

15. Cf. *Masses Ouvrières, art. cit.* October, 1960, p. 40.

to the calls of others. Until the Friend judges it opportune to come by surprise upon us....

In the light of the Parousia, the law of Christ thus appears to us as a law of eternal love, nourished in religion, for translation through justice into *the service of others* in an ascent of hope to Christ. It is the law of *growth* for a world called to become what it is—totally in accordance with the Spirit of liberty and of charity in order to be totally for Christ, and through Him, totally for the Father.

CONCLUSION

We have thus revealed in the Mystery of Christ manifested through His *mysteries*—Easter, Pentecost and the supreme Epiphany of God among men—all the fundamental characteristics of our morality: the Paschal law and the law of the Covenant; the law of the Spirit, the law of the Church, and the law of charity, with its twofold mediations, religious and fraternal.

Before considering these characteristics one by one we shall go carefully into their origin. Should a priest conclude from this chapter that the feasts of Easter, Pentecost or the Manifestation of the Lord would seem to provide every encouragement for a "moralizing" sermon? On the contrary, nothing could be more inappropriate if it be true that "the baptized *who is in Christ* ignores all morality provided that he has attained a certain stage of spiritual maturity."[16] What must be done is to proclaim the mystery of our union with God in Jesus Christ without fear of proclaiming thereby an ideal which is too lofty, since there must be

16. C. Spicq, *op. cit.*, p. 67.

announced at the same instant the Good News that grace is at work to accomplish this in us.

Each one of the demands, the details of which will follow, is thus only the obverse side of a grace. We are involved in the mysteries of Christ: in *faith* in the mystery of *Easter;* in the *charity* of *Pentecost;* in the *hope* of the *Parousia.*

Part II
In Faith in the Mystery
of Easter

A vertical line, a horizontal line . . . .

In the light of Christ our morality is situated at the intersection of these two lines.

It is—like the risen Jesus—the perfect response of love to the Father, **a dialogical morality, a morality of encounter,** a vertical reference to God (Chapter IV).

It possesses this reference only by historical liaison with Jesus Christ, by participation in His "passage" to the Father. It takes its place with Him in the **story of salvation.** Every instant of every day is given to it as an instant of grace, a call to emerge from egoism, a call to daily conversion, in two-fold horizontal reference to the first Coming of Christ and to His return (Chapter V).

CHAPTER FOUR

THE LAW OF CHRIST, A LAW OF THE NEW COVENANT

The supernatural end assumes the natural end and carries it out. We are naturally capable of responding to God, and we are supernaturally "called" by Him, and "justified" and "glorified" (cf. Rom. VIII, 30). All this is in Christ: "... when we give glory to God, it is through him that we say our Amen" (II Cor. I, 20) and it is through Him that *we shall enter therefore into that glory*. To be united with Christ is to answer *Yes* to God.

What we must do is to take up this Paschal basis and testify to its major importance by putting it back into all *aspects of the covenant* (I). It is going to provide us with the *ruling principle of Christian morality* (II). It is not enough to know it—it must be made part of one's life. In us too the *community ripens slowly* (III).

I. THE DIALOGUE OF LOVE BETWEEN GOD AND MEN

The Image of God

"Let us make man to our image and likeness" (Gen. I, 26).

"This theme of the image of God," states Etienne Gilson,

"is perhaps the dominant theme of Christian anthropology."[1] For us in the West the term "image" has become debased. An image is something which is little more than a pale and artificial representation of the reality. The Greeks, and the Fathers of the Church in general, had a much richer conception of the word image. An image is not a poor carbon copy, but a visible projection of the invisible reality. So, in so far as he is the image of God, man is a God of the earth, a God upon the earth, a likeness of God and, therefore, *an interlocutor* whom God procures for Himself, His "respondent," the one who can hear the words of God and can answer Him.

So we have the picture of Yahweh walking in the afternoon air with His children in paradise (Gen. III, 8).

Covenant with Israel

Man broke this dialogue but God, in His mercy, determined patiently to renew it throughout the course of history.

He gives a Word of promise to Abraham. And Abraham believes Him. He walks before God. He makes his life a *faithful response* to the Word of God. The peoples of the earth will be blessed in him. This is the commencement of an immense epic of the divine Word mingling with our words.

God reveals His Name to Moses, as a Friend to His friend. And His Word is not empty; it delivers Israel from Egypt. It assembles the People in the desert, already an image of the Church.

▄▄▄▄▄▄▄▄▄▄▄▄▄▄▄

1. The proof of this statement is found in many recent studies on this theme in the theology of the Fathers of the Church.

It is a Word of effective love, but, therefore, it is also exacting: "I am the Lord thy God, who brought thee out of the land of Egypt.... Thou shalt not have strange gods before me" (Exod. XX, 1-2). We realize that the *Decalogue*—the "Ten Words"—do no more than define the logical framework of the Covenant. The whole life of Israel will have to develop as a response of love to these words of life.

... And so resound the messages repeated by the prophets: "The Word of the Lord God," "The Word of Yahweh was given to me in these terms," "Listen to what the Lord God says...." And they predict that one day God will write His Word in the hearts of the faithful (Jer. XXXI, 31-34), and give them a new Spirit within them for an interior dialogue (Ezech. XXXVI, 26-27).

"And the Word was made flesh"

The covenant of God and humanity reaches its supreme fulfillment in Jesus Christ, in the marriage of the Eternal Word and our flesh. "God, who, at sundry times and in divers manners, spoke in times past to the fathers by the prophets, last of all, in these days hath spoken to us by his Son" (Heb. I, 1-2). Here is He who will govern our entire life. This is not a question of some new principle but of a fact: it is God who is there calling us and inviting us to follow Him in His Paschal mystery. Quite literally *the Father has given us His Word in order to bring us together in the Spirit of His love.*

Thus, on Easter morning, the Word of God and the response of man are supremely intertwined. The flesh finds itself assimilated in the fullness of the glory of the Word (John XVII, 5; cf. Coloss. II, 9).

The Church; the "holy Assembly of the Faithful"

The Church, which in Bossuet's words is "Jesus extended and communicated" is therefore the living Word . . . .

Its very name is another word for "assembly." The Church of Christ is the "gathering all together of the widely dispersed children of God," a gathering convoked by the Word of the Cross, a gathering which is itself a call. In the twofold sense of the "called" and the "caller" the Church is here on earth the "holy convocation" (Rom. I, 7; I Cor. 1, 2).

The eternal colloquy

This earthly Church directs us towards the heavenly Church. There the perfect community will be consummated. We must once and for all clear our minds of a mundane conception of Paradise. Heaven will not be an everlasting round of pleasure, but a personal cohabitation with God, *an ineffable participation in the colloquy of the Trinity*.

"So the profound unity of the saving plan of God and its harmony with our nature becomes clear: 'Father, Son and Spirit, God is for ever the Word, the eternal Word' and 'not any Word but a Word exhaling love,' the Word of Love. He has, in this Word, created man in His own image; man is an animal who speaks and whose word aspires to be an intimate word, a word of love. Man is fulfilled in communication, in exchange, in dialogue. He finds himself, as a result, inherently capable of entering into a dialogue with God Himself, if God so wishes to become his interlocutor. In this will he attain his highest perfection."[2]

2. B. Häring, *La Loi du Christ*, t. 1, 4th ed. p. 68.

It is clear too that there is no necessity to seek else-
where for the principle of his morality. Man's life must
be a response to God.

II. A MORALITY OF DIALOGUE

First of all let us get rid of inadequate conceptions of
Christian morality. Then we shall be able to see how
dogma invites us to consider the true criteria of morality.

1. *Inadequate Definitions*

A morality of the attainment of heavenly bliss?

Many reviews of the first volume of *The Law of Christ*
expressed regret that a work on morality did not commence
with a treatise on the last end. Father Häring deliberately
replaced it by a study on the community of man (which
he calls the "governing idea of moral theology").[3]
We should remember, too, that the treatise on the last
end in St. Thomas's thought is tightly bound up with the
treatise on God which precedes it—our "last end" is not
just some supreme Good, it is the living God. The study
on the community of God with man has the advantage of
giving its true name and its proper aspect to our last end
which is God the Father—attained in the Son—through the
Holy Spirit.
Above all it must not happen that the treatise on the

----

3. He gives his explanation of it in the *Supplément à la Vie Spirituelle*,
May 15, 1960, pp. 121-129. See also *La Loi du Christ*, t. 1, 4th ed. pp.
65-66.

last end should succeed in assessing our Christian morality as a eudemonist morality (i.e. a morality of happiness) like that of Aristotle. We are not pursuing our happiness before all else (God, in that event, being only a supplementary and superior means of achieving it); God is not the means of anything, not even that of attaining my happiness. I seek God for God Himself; in responding to His word, I am traveling along the road which leads to the encounter which will be eminently happy for me, but this will be something over and above.

"In the Christian perspective," as the Thomist philosopher Jacques Maritain puts it so excellently, "there is a decentering which means that the traditional designation, 'Ethic of Beatitude' (or of the last end), is only justified on condition that this Beatitude is understood as the happiness which unites both the complete fulfillment of all I could desire, though as the second goal, and, as the *first goal,* the transforming union with Another than I, whom I love more than myself, into whose life I enter for the full accomplishment of His Will."[4]

Père Le Guillou, O.P., who quotes this text, observes: "This is a truth which is, too often perhaps, left in obscurity."[5] It is our business to see that it does not remain there.

A Morality of Virtues?

Is Christian morality a *morality of virtues?* Yes, but its dominant character is not perhaps to be found in virtue, nor is its main activity, as certain writers seem to think,

---

4. *Neuf leçons sur les notions premières de la philosophie,* by J. Maritain, Paris, 1951, p. 22.

5. J. Le Guillou, Bulletin thomiste, No. 2 (1952), 627.

to be making the difficult choice between a scheme of
virtues and a scheme of the Commandments.   A morality
of virtues was primarily a pagan and stoic morality; a morality of virtues, to be Christian, must be supported by the
revelation of the word of God, by the "ten words," or
Commandments.   For virtues to appear in their Christian
guise they must be engraved on our hearts as our response
to the words of God.

A Morality of the Ideal?

May one speak of an "ideal Christian morality?"   Yes,
on the condition, however, of the "ideal" remaining "Christian" and of its not sinking into the Platonism of "ideas."   Our
ideal is a living one—it is the living Word of God incarnated
in Christ the Lord.   Besides, Christ is not a Confucius or
a superior Socrates.   Our pursuit of the ideal is a response
to Someone.

2. The True Criteria of a Christian Morality

God has spoken to us with love; our morality must be a
response to His Word, a dialogue, love for Love; a morality
of the Word and a morality of the Spirit.

A "dialogical" morality

Studying the *soul of Israel,* A. Gelin has perfectly characterized the morality of Revelation:
"It is essentially a morality of community; it takes the
form, therefore, of a dialogical structure; it is call and
response in the rhythm of a drama of which we know the
protagonists .... Biblical morality is not a humanist con-

struction, a technique of personal achievement and of social balance. It is part of the structure of the divine word being accepted or rejected. It assumes a summoning of man by God. The human response is one of obedience or of refusal."[6]

"Our life," as Fr. Häring will say in his turn, "develops henceforward in the form a response to a call."[7]

When one reflects upon what distinguishes the consciousness of a believer from that of an unbeliever (this comparison can help the former to appreciate the riches of his faith), one can, it would seem, state that the unbeliever is essentially aware of a solitude. His life is of the *monologic type;* he envisages it as something to be lived quite alone, counts solely upon himself to direct him to good, is aware that he is responsible to himself alone. Is not this what tht American convert Dorothy Day has demonstrated in her book *The Long Solitude* when she describes how her life moved along in solitude until the day she encountered the living God?

The believer is someone who has encountered God, or rather, someone into whose life one day God entered. "And now, all at once, you are Someone," cries Claudel. Immediately the dialogue is begun which will continue throughout that life; for God is not simply Someone who is waiting for me at the end of the route, and who is going to judge me on the last day; He is Someone who, every day, has something to say to me. Henceforth if I consider my life it is in terms of that Other; if I want to give my life a certain "form" it is because of Him; to shape my life I rely on Him. "I live in dialogue."

6. *L'âme d'Israël dans le Livre,* by A. Gelin, Paris 1958, pp. 31-33.
7. *La Loi du Christ,* B. Häring, t. 1, 4th ed. pp. 73-76.

94

It is with the believer as with the lover who has encountered the girl of his heart—his life is turned upside down. Up to this he was alone even in the midst of others; henceforth he has taken cognizance of himself (his encounter has been a personal thing) and he now contemplates his life in terms of the other person. So with the Christian who has found God "as one encounters a friend in the evening at the corner of the street;"[8] his life is no longer a destiny which is insipid or devoid of meaning, nor is it an impersonal fate. It is a route outlined by Someone who calls us by walking before us. I exist from now on with Him. He expects from me a certain kind of life. Nothing of what goes to make up my life is unimportant to Him; and I must live for His glory by responding to His desires.

This encounter is often a struggle—the struggle of Jacob and the Angel. That mysterious page of Genesis has inspired commentaries by many spiritual writers. Our life unfolds in the night of faith: every day there is the encounter of Jacob and God. He attacks, we repel, we struggle, we fight. But from the start of this encounter we are marked, we have become Israel, the man of God, the man for God. God Himself has become God for us (Yahweh, God of Israel). We live our life together, the Lord remaining the Lord, of course.

A Morality of Charity

"Christian morality is an ethic of charity, absolutely passed over by the religious history of the world; a life developing as a dialogue of love."[9]

8. Lacordaire, *Conférences de Toulouse*, 1854.
9. *La Loi du Christ* B. Häring, t. 2, p. 17.

This is undoubtedly the driving idea of mediaeval theology. We might need to go a little further than the inevitable changes in the meaning of words which occur in the course of time to find again the full abundance of meaning which this word charity held for the Middle Ages. Daringly assimilating Aristotle, and transcending him, St. Thomas, the heir of St. Augustine, looks upon charity as a *friendship* with God.

When we think about grace or charity we are too apt to consider them as things, unspecific, impersonal things. We must not let ourselves be caught and held by simple impressions. Grace and charity are not things, they are an awakening of the human personality to God—man has become the friend, the intimate of God, who sees God and treats Him as a friend. And what is this friendship if not unceasing dialogue and personal exchange? All man's activities are as it were permeated and transformed by it, all the Christian "virtues" derive from this charity-friendship which is their "form." That is the essential word, but unfortunately we no longer appreciate all the richness which the theologians of the Middle Ages included in this technical word. Fr. Gilleman has recently tried to recall it to us in *The Primacy of Charity in Moral Theology.*

A Christian life may be said to be "informed" by charity when it becomes fully animated and impregnated by charity to the point of being no longer anything but a succession of gestures and acts of *friendship.* Our actions without charity are no more than "detached fragments" which have no significance for salvation. It is charity which coordinates them into a unity, sets them all moving in the same direction, confers a meaning upon them by making them all contribute to our last end. Charity will animate and complete all our acts of virtue. All these actions emanating from different virtues will be "mediations," all will be means and privileged signs of charity alone; they will all (without losing their individual nature) become gestures of love in response to the God of love, and they will deepen our intimacy with God. It is clear that we are always in the same personal climate; Christian life does not develop through fidelity to principles, excellent though they be, but through fidelity to Another, to God who calls man to His friendship.

A morality which is essentially religious

To sum up, one can say that our Christian morality is essentially *religious*. It is not a matter of acquiring a morality for man and for the perfection of man, independent of man's religious relation with God. Although there is obviously a necessity to pay attention to a primary Table of the Law (the first three Commandments of the Decalogue) governing our attitudes towards God, and a secondary Table (the remaining seven Commandments) the first should not be defined as *sacred* and the second as *profane* (or at best sanctioned from the outside by religion as Rudolf Otto conceives it).

In reality *our whole morality is theological*. God, for me, is not simply One who comes to sanction my moral life from the outside, who is waiting for me at the corner of the road as a policeman waits for someone who has just broken the law; very much more is He the One who inspires my entire life from within, dominates it and builds it up with me. In a Christian life nothing is purely profane, everything is made sacred, everything is directed towards God, everything gives Him glory and radiates His holiness. "It is just as noble to peel potatoes for the love of God as to build cathedrals."

This impregnation of morality by the theological life is so profound that one would be right to say with Père Liégé: "Really, although paradoxically, there is no morality in Christianity; there is a faith in the Christian mystery which transforms the life of the believer."[10]

III. CATECHETICAL AND PASTORAL ORIENTATIONS

A *Progressive Education*

Man is a being in the course of development.

Making his moral life a dialogue with God presupposes a certain maturity of faith, to which he accedes by successive stages. Educators know that the average child begins with a legal morality, the categorical imperative; the good is what Mamma and Daddy have said. The adolescent conceives morality as an ideal, an ideal development of his personality. He will accede only very slowly to the final stage—a morality of encounter with God and of dialogue.

A *Journey Fraught With Perils*

These mutations, a feature of natural growth, contain many dangers of blockage, of regression or of deviation.

For a child his father and mother are the mouthpiece of God. Conforming to their wishes through love is—within the scope of childhood—living a dialogical morality.

For the adolescent who must win his freedom this tutelage quickly becomes a constraint. He wants to develop

----

10. *Avent à Saint-Séverin*, 1955, p. 8. Cf. *Vivre en chrétien*, 1960, p. 14.

his own individuality. He would not refuse to designate God as the Absolute of perfection which attracts him and for Whom he even dreams of pouring himself out generously in sacrifice. But he rejects social conformity, ready-made morality, custom, the conventions. If one should ever persist in showing God to him only through the tangle of those external imperatives, one would run the very grave risk that he will in addition reject this demanding Legislator, who is only a superior policeman of a morality which constrains and bullies him.

One can see his dilemma. Many resolve it, temporarily at least, by revolt, by anarchy, only, at the end of a few years sowing wild oats, so to speak, to pull themselves up and then very quickly adopt a bourgeois morality, a morality of external manifestation of greater or lesser hypocrisy, where life is constantly a matter of keeping up a facade—a morality, in other words, of Pharisaical observances. However social it may be called, such a morality has nothing altruistic about it—its total value amounts to no more than the common denominator of the egoism of everyone. It is unnecessary to say that such a morality is not Christian, even if it coincides externally with a certain number of the requirements of Christianity.

Others insist on the non-conformist declaration of their singularity:

André Gide:

"My parents had accustomed me to act not according to the dictates of my own nature, but according to a moral rule exterior to me, one which they considered applicable to all men."[11]

"But it began to seem to me, rather, that duty was not

11. *Journal,* By André Gide, p. 775.

the same for every individual and that God Himself might well have a horror of such uniformity against which nature rebelled but towards which, it seemed to me, the ideal Christian veered by pretending to overcome nature. I admitted no more than particular morals sometimes presenting conflicting commands. So that every attempt to submit oneself to a common rule became treason in my eyes." [12]

No route sketched in advance! No prefabricated morality! No ready-made rules!

In fact, as far as the adolescent is concerned, the only possible choice would seem to be either the hypocrisy of *convention* or the immorality of *revolt*.

The Christian Solution

In fact there is a possible way around this because both of these attitudes are vitiated by egoism. The answer is born of *dedicated* love. It is a matter of finding other people and above all of finding Another, not in the shape of an anonymous Legislator but in the form of the One who needs my particular love and my free response. Liberty, sincerity, community—we shall show how all these values are not only safeguarded but enlarged by Christian morality.

We admit, however, that it is not enough to *preach* this meaning of the dialogue and of charity. We must insert it into society and never overlook the fact that the authentic accomplishment of charity in action can be born only of an interior and convinced adherence to it. Charity ought to be encouraged, but one cannot insist that a ready-made suit of it be put on. God begins the change in a man from within. He works from the inside by giving His grace to the

----

12. *By André Gide, Si le grain ne meurt*, p. 274.

inmost recesses of the person. It is only at a very slow pace that conversion moves from the interior to the exterior. To want to proceed in any other fashion is not in conformity with the wishes and the procedure of God; and that involves the possibility of dangerous regressions in the future. The needs of a morality of Covenant can only be born of belief in this Covenant. An educator must be convinced always *of the primacy of faith for the living of a moral life.*

CHAPTER FIVE

THE LAW OF CHRIST, THE LAW OF DAILY CONVERSION

The whole story or history of Christ is one of a "passage" into the Glory of His Father. Each one of our destinies is inscribed in this *history,* in this *Passover.*

This divine disposition to center everything upon Easter (I), governs our morality: to live in conformity with the law of Christ is not only to live according to the rule of eternal norms, but is also to be in harmony with a history, to be involved in a mighty Passover (II). Such a conversion is both the work of a moment and the work of every moment (III).

I. THE PASSOVER OF CHRIST, THE KEY TO HISTORY

We become

The renewal of the Paschal mystery has set in motion in the Christian consciousness an increased sense of becoming. The reflections and studies of theologians have in these latter years been multiplied upon what has very properly been called the *mystery of history.*[1] It has been

---

1. We recall Daniélou's excellent *Essai sur le Mystère de l'Histoire,* Paris 1952, and Chifflot's *Approches pour une Théologie de l'Histoire,* Paris 1960: and from the Protestant theologians, O. Cullman, *Christ et le Temps,* 1947.

persistently said and repeated that the order of salvation, while it is an eternal work of God, develops for us in historical stages. *Our Credo is a history.* The Lord comes. Salvation is built into time.

It is not certain that these statements have yet revealed all that they imply. Between the Platonic philosophers who despair of history, and the facile myths of Marxism with its idolatry of temporal progress, it is our business to examine the following truth with ever increasing concentration and depth—our Credo is not solely a *history,* it is *profound and true history.*

Republics succeed each other, empires crumble, civilizations acknowledge mortality, the map of the world changes like the landscape from snow to spring; across these superficial vicissitudes—across the destiny of every individual man—God pursues His plan. He constructs history, the history which must endure. At the close of this plan of salvation will appear *the celestial Jerusalem,* the fruit of the perishable centuries, and this, for all men, will be an imperishable communion of love with God. Such is the divine objective, the marvellous reality which gives its meaning to history.

We become free

This communion of eternal love can only be a free communion of hearts; concerned as it is with men, it assumes the maturing of their liberties. How long will history last? As long, Origen calculates,[2] as will be necessary for our human liberties to be educated.

----

2. Cf. *Origène* by J. Daniélou, Paris 1948, p. 203.

For him the earth is one immense school: the course of study will last as long as is necessary—once our liberties have matured—for God to examine and evaluate the responses. One could say as much of each one of our personal histories. When we have found or refound our lost liberty, when it is completely "released" through charity, then we shall have completed our classes, completed our lives. This vast movement which leads us *from the liberty enslaved by sin to the liberty released by charity*, is the education of sinful humanity by the Providence of God.

It must be added that this history is a battlefield, a confrontation, through us, between God and Satan—Satan, the seducer of human liberty, and Christ the liberator of our enslaved liberties. Tugged between the appeals of each of them man must make his own choice. He is involved in the *No* with Satan through Adam and sinful humanity of which he is a part; he must be involved in the *Yes* with God through Jesus Christ. History in its profound and invisible reality is the history of our choice of Good or of Evil; a reality more durable than the history which is visible and obvious, and related from day to day in the papers and recorded in our textbooks.

God builds history, we said. Let us say rather that He gives it to us to build. He puts it up to us to win our liberties throughout history for the eternal communion of love.

We become free in Jesus Christ

We know all this, and we have confidence in Jesus Christ. In the eyes of our faith, a decisive event took place, an event which gives its meaning to the whole of history, which positively orientates it—Christ, the Incarnate Son of God, *died and rose again from the dead*. This is the Paschal mystery. This death of expiation, and this resurrection has marked for ever the defeat of the devil who is allied to sin and death, and the victory of all who adhere to Christ through faith. History henceforth possesses in itself a center of reference and of attraction for liberty which is sought and can be found only in God. Inclined towards the egotistical and the sterile *No*, because of the weight of sin, *this liberty is now drawn towards the Yes by the grace of the Risen One*.

The Paschal mystery will thus ensure the success of real history over the chaos of apparent history: it involves, in the liberty of the children of God, the "passage" of that humanity of which Christ is the innocent and dedicated first fruit. The risen Christ dominates history; He carries it, and, as Karl Barth says, he "carries it along" towards eternity.

He will return to ensure the resounding triumph of all those who shall have chosen to live according to His charity. "The history of the Church and of the Christian receives its coordinates from the first and second coming of Christ."[3] This history only makes any sense because it is borne mysteriously along by the first coming of the Lord towards His return, from the Passover to the Parousia. Such are its two poles. Such is its axis which fixes the "today" of our faith. How is it possible for us to believe casually that

3. B. Häring, *La Loi du Christ*, 1, p. 134.

106

this view of faith has no bearing on our morality, when what is at stake, to the very eyes of that faith, is the time of our liberty?

II. A PASCHAL MORALITY

Since moral catechesis keeps before us the kerygma, the good news of God's salvation brought about by the Passover of Christ brings us to this conclusion—we live in the logic of this Passover which has already been accomplished, we are sustained by the life of the Risen One who is carrying us towards the eternal Passover, we are living this "passage" today.

In other words we live the story of the Church in time which the Eucharist sums up: *Recolitur memoria passionis ejus*: We commemorate His passion (cf. "Wherefore... calling to mind... O Lord"); *Mens impletur gratia*: The soul is filled with grace (cf. "This day have I begotten thee....", "Today if you shall hear his voice...."); *Et futurae gloriae nobis pignus datur*: Pledge given to us of future glory (cf. "Until he come," "Come, Lord Jesus, come)".

We are rooted in the *past* and extended towards the *future* in the grace of today, unique and ineffable.

1. *A Morality of the Past?*

Christ yesterday

The Lord delivered us in accordance with human logic. He became Man. He knew the weight of memory in our lives—the memory of the dead; the lessons of the past. He took all that into His reckoning. He fixed the event of sal-

107

vation once (*hapax!* Heb. IX, 28; I Pet. III, 18) in the
fulness of time, He appointed a time when humanity had
become sufficiently mature to understand it and capable
of preserving the memory of it. It was His desire that our
entire lives should be a commemoration of that event. So
previously had the Hebrews commemorated Exodus and
the Passover. For us, our Passover is Christ. We live within
this memory. In one sense, according to Cullmann's dictum,
one cannot "pass over the Passover of Christ."

Our whole Christian morality springs from it. For it
gave birth to the sacraments of Christ. Now each one of
these sacraments brings us back to the Passover. They
are all, springing from baptism and relating to the Eucharist,
sacraments of the Passover of Christ. We have here a
strange subordination and one which is inconceivable for
pure philosophers. Our morality, instead of being meas-
ured directly against timeless values, claims to have its
roots in the past. Yet the truth is that it draws therefrom an
ever-new vitality—the vitality of the "passage" from death
to life.

Death and Resurrection

If eternal life is knowing Christ as St. John says (XVII,
3), we may define it precisely with Paul: "... to know him,
and the power of his resurrection, and the fellowship of his
sufferings, being made conformable to his death, if by any
means I may attain to the resurrection which is from the
dead" (Phil. III, 10-11). It is in this mystery of death
and of resurrection that we are immersed through baptism
(cf. Rom. VI, 3-4).

The reference to the past does not therefore take us
back to a fixed point but to a movement, a change—an up-

rooting from sin for a grafting on to the Lord, a conversion. *If the Passover is the key to history, this Paschal conversion is the key to Christian morality.*

Our morality is a morality of conversion and oblation.

The daily conversion

This conversion is not only imperative for the first moment of our moral existence, it matters for all the days of our lives. We are in constant contact with this movement which derives from the past and to which we are committed by baptism, just as points on a circumference are related to their center.

All the sacraments received after baptism lead us back to this conversion, especially and above all the sacrament of penance, the "second baptism" as the Fathers call it.... May frequent confession preserve for us its fundamental sense of that paschal movement: the return of the Prodigal Son, uprooting himself from his humiliating existence as a swineherder to return to his Father; plunged into the death of Christ in order to rise again to life in the house of God.

The Christian's life should be, according to an author who was highly regarded not so very long ago, a "daily conversion."[4] Happy the man who can live it beginning with daily Mass, provided, of course that this has not become a routine affair! O desolation! O human frailty! Every one of our Masses is the celebration of a unique

----

4. *La conversion chrétienne,* by A. Desurmont, Edition Riblier, Paris 1910.

event, of a hapax: "Wherefore...calling to mind...O Lord...!" And we can turn the commemoration of the ineffable into a banality! Though the Mass is there to transfigure, every day, the banality of our lives into the ineffable Passover!

For the paschal movement is started in Christ Jesus for ever and it forces us unwearyingly towards the future.

2. A Morality of the Future?

In former times preachers of retreats or parish missions put very considerable emphasis upon the last things. And it is not because these "great truths" can now be more fully understood in the light of the mystery of Christ that one should criticize those who taught them with the theology they possessed; they were in this the witnesses of an authentic value of Christianity, namely eschatology. Père Congar complains that Christian morality is not sufficiently impregnated and elevated by the eschatological current.[5]

Christian morality has indeed essentially the outlook of the Parousia, it leans towards the return of the Lord, not only because this return will be the sanction of our lives, but chiefly because death alone (for each one of us) and the return of Christ (for the whole of humanity) will bring about the assimilation of our being (or of all the redeemed) with the risen Christ. Without ever resting upon the work done, we must see our lives under the sign of an ascent up to that zenith, that action which is the highest we shall ever be able to accomplish, namely, our death.

▀▀▀▀▀▀▀▀▀▀▀▀▀▀

5. In *Le Mystère de la Mort et sa celebration,* Paris 1951, Y. Congar's chapter, p. 312.

It is Blondel who defines death as "the highest action, this most complete passion," because it will truly be the most beautiful imitation of Christ in His paschal mystery. At my death I shall reach my eternal measure in Christ, I shall become totally like to Him, risen in the Risen One.

A movement forward

Our morality, fully impregnated with an eschatological dynamism, is therefore a morality in progress, in movement (St. Paul spoke even of forgetting the things that are behind, and stretching forth to those that are before), although sometimes it gives the impression of moving at a jog-trot, of marking time or even of trying to lag behind.

In other words, there is a certain tension, a certain dynamism characteristic of Christian moral life which is explained by this movement towards the encounter with (and at the same time towards the "following of") the risen Christ, which means that the Christian life is quite different from simple humanism. One might say that the humanist, by definition, is not urged in such a way. He wants to enjoy life to the full, not to consume it too quickly; he is not in any hurry to die. This "natural" sentiment seems to have vanished from the hearts of the saints: ever since St. Paul they have become people who press on, people who are hastening to the encounter with the Lord!

If we had this desire in our hearts to find the Lord again we should take more seriously every day as it came. We know the wonderful words St. Ignatius of Antioch uses in his letter to the Romans asking them not to oppose his martyrdom: "Suffer me to be the food of wild beasts ... that I may happily make my way to Jesus Christ .... Once arrived there I shall be a man."[6] Does this nostalgia "to be with Christ," this tension of hope, still impregnate our moral life?

3. A Morality of "God's Today"

Are we then suspended between the past and the future, the beneficiaries of a salvation *already* won, but not *yet* revealed, so that the present moment must, as such, be devoid of interest? A whole section of Protestantism inclines towards this conception and minimizes the actual and current presence of grace, the direct and current efficacy of the sacraments, the actual and current mediation of the Church.

Christ today

However,—and this is a sign of the times—a Protestant, Pastor Schutz of Taizé, has brought out a book under the significant title, *Living God's Today.*

In fact it is the psalms, the liturgy, which speak to us constantly of "God's today," the *hodie*: *"Today, if you would hear his voice, harden not your hearts"* (Ps. XCIV, 8); *"Hodie salvator apparuit;" "Behold, I am with you all days"* (Matt. XXVIII, 20). All days, and therefore today.

The past has been given to us once and for all: Easter is *still* there. The future was inaugurated from the moment of the Resurrection and the Parousia is inscribed in advance

▬▬▬▬▬▬▬▬▬▬▬▬▬▬

6. St. Ignatius of Antioch, *Letter to the Romans*, VI.

112

in all the triumphs of the Church, great or small; it is *already* there. At the intersection of what is permanent and what is anticipated, every day is the today of Christ who offers Himself to us sacramentally in order to be welcomed by us in our brethren. "Whatever you do to the least of my little ones;" the Eucharistic presence and the presence of our neighbor; *Christus hodie.*

"Le bel aujourd'hui"

In these circumstances there is no question for the Christian of escaping from the present. Platonists, Manichaeans, Quietists, all in their turn, declaring that present existence is mediocre, evil or sterile, took refuge in the expectation of another existence. Taking them all in all, the *carpe diem* of the Epicureans is less insulting to the Lord, for every day is for us the "haec dies," "this day which the Lord has made:" a paschal present. If we do not gather from it "the roses of life" we find in it again the "marvels of God" (the sacraments, the charisms, the miracles—above all, holiness) which make of all future history, of all life, *a holy history.*

Every year is a "year of grace," dated from Christ, every day is a day of grace in which the Passover of Christ bears fruit for His eternal return. With what love, even if the time is grey and our hearts sullen, we can salute every morning in Mallarmé's line:

"Le vierge, le vivace et le bel aujourd'hui"[7] since the Lord gives us a rendezvous in it. Every hour is an hour of grace, a "Kairos," a holy time, even if it does not appear to hold anything sensational, because divine grace and hu-

----

7. This is also the title of a book by J. Green: *Le bel aujourd'hui.*

man liberty are collaborating in it for the erection of the Eternal City.

"Time is money," say the English. Oh yes! Look what it cost my Savior when His hour was come. It is the hour precious as a rare pearl, because the treasure of the Kingdom is contained in it. It is the hour in which it is necessary to watch because the thief comes. "The present moment," says Père de Caussade, "is the manifestation of the name of God and the advent of His reign."[8] *Christus hodie.*

God speaks through events

"If God gave us rulers of His own choosing, Oh, how essential it would be to obey them willingly! Necessity and events are certainly connected."[9] Each hour brings us its necessity, and minute or important, its events. God speaks to us through them.

"God reveals Himself to us," says Père de Caussade again, "in the most common events in a manner as mysterious but as real and as adorable as in the great events of history and in the holy Scriptures."[10] It is not a stereotyped behavior which is therefore demanded of us, but a new response at every moment, since at every moment God is speaking to us.

A morality of situation?

Is one to conclude from this that all general morality should be repudiated in order to rely on the suggestions of

8. *Abandonment to Divine Providence* by J. P. de Caussade.
9. *Le Mystère de Jesus* by Pascal.
10. *Op. cit.* by J. P. de Caussade.

114

the moment, on what the situation calls for, according to our free interpretation of it?

Right from the start, of course, there is a well-founded prejudice against the formula known as the "morality of the situation," because of the abuse of it by non-Christian existentialists, something which leads to the ruin of all objective morality; also because of Protestantism which, especially in Germany, has preached it widely. But while the expression, "situation ethics," is relatively new (1930), and while the abuses we have mentioned are notorious and were condemned by Pius XII in 1952 and by the Holy Office in 1956, the reality is profoundly traditional in the Church, for it is linked to the *dogma of the Holy Spirit*.

The Tradition of the Church

Ever since the Church has been the Church she has believed in the inspiration of the Holy Spirit; she believes in a personal call from God to each one of us, or, to use the language of Scripture, she believes that God calls us "by our name" and knows us intimately. Everyone, in consequence, has his original vocation, his indispensable route to travel before God.

Even the most "moralizing" of the moralists in the heyday of casuistry (the 17th and 18th centuries) have been basically preoccupied with the application of the objective moral laws to circumstances or to particular cases. And their moral systems (which disturb us by their complex profusion—probabilism, probabiliorism, equiprobabilism, etc.) were created with the profound intention of keeping as close as possible to concrete data in order to see how, in precise circumstances, the law might be applied in a way which would both respect

115

the liberty of human individuals and their fidelity to certain calls from God.

The three circles

How, in actual fact, are we to know just what God expects from us at a precise moment in our personal history? One might outline it as follows: there is, in the first place, fidelity to the Church and to her magisterium, which as the authentic interpreter of the Law and of the Gospel presents the Christian viewpoints of mankind. Then there is fidelity to the more particular call of circumstances, of the occasion.

To employ an image, we might think of this in the form of *two concentric circles*: the first, the larger, represents the morality of natures, of essences, of general laws, of values. The second, inside the first, would represent a certain approach from a Christian understanding of the situation: every pastor of souls is bound to try to make out a parallel case and every Christian desirous of perfection tries to do as much in his own way, even if, like Monsieur Jourdain, he does not know he is doing so.

But that much said, we should now add a third, smaller circle which would in actual fact encircle what is unique and original in the situation. It would have value only to the extent to which it is registered in the first two circles;[11] but

11. The mistake of the atheistic existentialist (and to a lesser degree the mistake of the Protestant) is to deny the demands of the first two circles.

God really speaks there to each individual by mediation and the unique voice of his conscience. "The situation is a religious reality in which God and man are present to each other, in an "I-you" relationship, at a special moment which will never be repeated."[12]

"Veni, Domine Jesu. Veni, Sancte Spiritus"

The old scholastics said: "Individuum est ineffabile," "the individual is ineffable." One cannot express in general terms what characterizes and defines individual originality. In a certain way, too, we must say that the situation is not reducible integrally to a category, even a casuistic category. In this unique situation of my history who will make me truly accomplish the will of God? The answer is the Holy Spirit, expressing Himself in a conscience which has been made really sensitive to His call, because it has, previously, perfectly integrated the findings of a casuistic morality, as a morality of values, or of essences. Only this fully educated conscience, together with the Holy Spirit, can realize the vital synthesis of all the elements of a moment. That is why one can never really judge anyone; the Church herself does not recognize the right to judge the conscience of anyone in an absolute way. God alone is Judge.

"The wily person," writes Fr. Häring, "has the gift of seeing in reality what may serve his plans. The prudent person possesses as keen a lucidity as the wily one but it is for perceiving in the movement of humanity how he can turn everything to the service of good and finally to the service of God. But prudence, in fact, attains its perfection only

12. J. Fuchs, S.J., *Morale théologique et Morale de situation,* in *Nouvelle Rev. Théol.* 1954. p. 1076.

through the Holy Spirit who induces docility to the slightest interior movements of divine grace, as also to the demands of the situation. It is only through the Spirit that the soul penetrates to the full depths of the reality; henceforward in all things the soul hears the word, full of love, of her Lord and the invitation to filial service in charity."[13]

Between Easter and the Parousia the only person who can say with assurance in the today of God, "Come, Lord Jesus, come" is he who says with the Church, "Come, Holy Spirit, to subject me to Thy law."

III. CATECHETICAL AND PASTORAL ORIENTATIONS

The progressing Church, made up of progressing communities and of faithful moving towards God, are the people of whom we are the pastors, the educators or the friends. Let us never forget that they are subject to time.

Therefore, *patience*. Let us lead those who are entrusted to us at God's pace. *Confidence*, too. The Lord who is waiting for us at the end of the road spurs us on. *Discernment*. There are plenty of ways to join Him—all are not meant to follow the same path. Souls must be led to Him according to the indication He gives them through events.

Patience

Time was needed to educate humanity for the coming of the Lord. Time is likewise needed so that the Church, a single parish, a single soul may embark upon this Passover.

---

13. *La loi du Christ* by B. Häring, t. I, p. 428.

The progression is not necessarily linear nor above all "geometrical." Even those lives which are truly ascending have moments of hesitation or of apparent stagnation, sometimes even falls, from which, however, there is no cause to draw dramatic conclusions. We judge according to appearances: the Lord, however, is patient. It is essential to try to imitate this divine "virtue," so admirable in St. Augustine's eyes. The Lord even knows how to draw good from evil. He has done so in human history. (See Pharaoh: after all we owe to him the resounding glory of the Exodus, "with a strong hand and a stretched out arm"). He does it in each and everyone of our lives, according to the Portuguese proverb cut on the reverse of the coin in "The Satin Slipper:" *"Deus escreve direito por linhas tortas,"* "God writes straight with crooked lines." Through this is not, at the same time, an invitation to make our roads tortuous at will! God alone knows the mystery of individuals and of freedoms, and such definitive judgments are very disquieting if issuing from certain priests or educators.

The law of growth is such that we can be brought to tolerate evil, and even to advise, in certain cases, something which lies below the objective norm of good and of the social demands of the Church, but which constitutes subjectively for the person who listens to us the best that is possible for today. God gave us examples in the Old Testament of this pedagogical prudence, of these merciful extensions.

Confidence

This is not a matter, moreover, of sinning by omission, by pusillanimity, under the pretext of imitating the divine patience and discretion. The law of growth does not mean

119

solely slowness in growth (the grain of mustard seed), but effective growth (the great tree). Christians must be invited to progress with courage and they must be given help. It is necessary to see each and everyone of them in the future of glory which awaits them, and consequently to spur them on. We must fear to retard a single soul in this metamorphosis to which the Passover is carrying it. We must fear to hold back a parish or a group where those of good will are searching and only awaiting a little more confidence in their possible initiatives. We must not deter them from such enterprise solely through fear of failure— the Cross leads to Glory. Engender trust in the Lord who is coming.

Discernment

Discernment of spirits, the understanding of what suits each one according to the events and the ability to help each one to make the revision of his life in this sense with lucidity and realism is a capital virtue in pastor or counsellor. Consciences are not made by God in categories. Each individual must be helped to discover the way of the Lord today, the way through which he can and must grow in the Church today.

Part III
In the Charity of Pentecost

Christian morality is the morality of the Spirit of Christ which has become our law. That is why it is, of course, **a morality of perfect liberty.** Do we give expression to such a morality, and do we truly desire to arouse Christians around us who are led by the Spirit? (Chapter VI).

As the mystery of Pentecost testifies, the Spirit is closely linked with the Church. Christian morality therefore must also be a morality of communal solidarity and of hierarchic submission; **the law of Christ, a law of the Church** (Chapter VII).

It is love—**the Spirit of love**—which wonderfully resolves this antinomy. But whom must we love, God or man? Beyond these dilemmas, which have bothered the legalists of all times, the mystery of the Church defines not only the framework of our morality, but its purport and its very essences, from which must derive both the most remote and the most immediate of its determinations: Christians, we are called to live and to make live the **Communion of Saints** (Chapter VIII).

CHAPTER SIX

THE LAW OF CHRIST: THE LAW OF THE SPIRIT

The law of the Christian is the law of community. The
Christian lives in the name of another. So faith ordains.
And we are saved, through our morality, from egoism.

But, it may be objected, are we not then returning to
subjection, to enslavement, to alienation? Surely to live
in the name of another is to abdicate one's own liberty.
How can our liberty be preserved within the framework of
a morality of faith? The word law has about it an air of
that which binds, a link, the word community has it also.
But links mean chains!

We speak of a "dialogical morality." This is a nice way
of putting it, for is it not God who frames both the questions
and the answers? One may give whatever version one likes
of one's call, the fact remains that it is God who determines
it, God who settles our vocations for us. We are petrified
beneath His gaze, our destinies planned as though we were
automatons, not to mention the fact that He knows perfectly
well the extent to which we can, or cannot, fulfill His plan.
So, it would seem, we have no need to discover our vocations
ourselves and, after all, is not this a more convenient arrangement?

The impasse of Christian morality

Jean Paul Sartre who jeers at bourgeois morality, where
everything we do is determined by human respect, by the

123

gaze of others which paralyzes us, denounces specifically the absolute formula in a morality based on the all-embracing gaze of God, the Other who sees me. He pushes the caricature to the extreme of odium in his Daniel of *Chemins de la liberté* ("Roads of Liberty").

"Daniel discloses the news of his conversion to Matthew: 'One moment, on that June evening when I decided to confess to you, I thought I could touch myself in your frightened eyes. You *saw* me, in your eyes I was solid and foreseeable; my actions and my dispositions were no more than the consequences of an appointed essence .... (But there is something better). God sees me, Matthew; I feel it, I know it. So, everything is said in one moment .... What anguish to discover this gaze suddenly like some universal milieu from whence I cannot make my escape. But what peace too. I know at last what I am ... I am seen, therefore I am. I no longer have to bear the responsibility of my own toneless existence: He who sees me makes me exist; I am as He sees me ....

"I went to see the parish priest of Sauveterre. He is a well-read and wily peasant, with the lined and mobile face of an elderly comedian. He did not exactly appeal to me, but he was not unpleasant, as my first contact with the Church through his intermediary had been. He received me in an office adorned with an array of books which surely he had not read ....

" 'Father,' I said to him, 'I only want some information: does your religion teach that God sees us?'

" 'He sees us,' he replied in surprise. 'He reads our hearts.'

" 'But what does He see?' I asked. 'Does He see this froth, that dross, out of which my daily thoughts are made up, or does His gaze rather penetrate to our eternal essence?'

"And the old fox gave me this answer, in which I recognized an ancient wisdom:

" 'Sir, God sees everything!' "[1]

What anguish and what peace! What petrification and what an alibi! It is true that Sartre, who claims to denounce our morality in such words as "an enslavement," has never achieved his own "Roads of Liberty." He admits being no longer able to see clearly where they lead.[2]

What is to be said of our liberty?

Are we in a similar impasse? Is not the morality which we have to preach only a law, the more paralyzing in that it is intensified by an implacable gaze?

Thank God the Scriptures expressly preserve us from this misconception. St. James calls the law of Christ "the perfect law of liberty" (I, 25; II, 12), and St. Paul proclaims "For the law of the spirit of life in Christ Jesus, hath delivered me from the law of sin and of death" (Rom. VIII, 2).

We have called it the Law of the Covenant. Let us put it precisely—the Law of the *New* Covenant. If the former Law was lived as a covenant according to the letter which paralyzes, the new Law is to be a covenant according to the Spirit who vivifies.

St. Thomas was not afraid to write: "The Spirit Himself as He generates in our souls the charity which is the perfect accomplishment of the law, is the New Covenant."[3]

----

1. *Les chemins de la liberté* by J. P. Sartre; II: *Le sursis,* pp. 318-320, *passim.*

2. Cf. excerpt quoted from *Critique de la raison dialectique* above, pp. 36-37.

3. *Comment. in 2 Cor. III,* 1-2.

And consequently: "The essential in the law of the New Testament, and the factor in which all its strength resides, is the grace of the Holy Spirit which is given through faith in Christ. And thus the New Law is principally the grace of the Holy Spirit Himself."[4]

Is this our conviction, and is it one of the principles of our attitude in respect of others? But do we believe truly from the outset in the role of the Holy Spirit in the system of salvation?

Let us recall our faith, then, since it commands our morality (I). We shall see better how our morality is a morality of the Spirit (II). We shall draw new and practical lessons from it (III).

I. THE SPIRIT OF CHRIST HAS BEEN GIVEN TO US

While the Greek theologians, even to this day, divide theology into three parts, "Patrology" (the study of the Omnipotent Father and Creator), "Christology" (the study of the Son, the Redeemer) and "Pneumatology" (the study of the Life-giving Spirit, which includes the Church and all morality), it is well to acknowledge that in Latin theology the Holy Spirit has often figured as the poor relation. It is as if this were a difficult zone into which it would seem preferable not to venture.

The Dogma of the Trinity

Our morality is a dialogue. But in whom then is the eternal dialogue betwen the Father and the Son established?

----

4. Ia - IIae, q. 106. a. 1.

In whom does the Son give Himself to the Father, in whom is the Father united with the Son? *"In unitate Spiritus Sancti."* In the Holy Spirit, the living link between the Father and Son, the witness and maker of their eternal meeting, the *impelling movement* which carries them One towards the Other, the torrential and irresistible force of love.

Christ, consummated in the Spirit through the Resurrection

St. Irenaeus, theologian of the system of salvation, (otherwise known as the progressive dispensation of the riches of salvation) sees at work in the world, for the gathering of men in God, *"the two hands of the Father,"* the Word and the Spirit, very closely associated. The Logos is at work since the beginning. But so is the Spirit. He is there since the very first creation, the breath of God upon the waters. It is He who speaks through the prophets. He helps the inspired writers. It is through Him that the Incarnation takes place: "Mary ... was found with child, of the Holy Spirit" (Matt. I, 18).

"The Spirit of the Lord is upon me," said Christ in His turn, and the commentators upon His earthly life show Him to us "urged by the Holy Spirit" and finally offering Himself, through Him, in sacrifice to the Father. In His state of kenosis, (or abandonment) as St. Paul says, (Phil. II, 7), His body had not yet been wholly filled with the strength of the Holy Spirit, which led Him to the Father. This is why, while Christ had personally lived up to then in the strength of the Holy Spirit, He had not yet communicated Him to men. "For as yet the Spirit was not given, because Jesus was not yet glorified" (John VII, 39). Only His Resurrection-Consecration, *the full sway of the Spirit over*

His being, made Him ontologically the perfect mediator of the return to the Father, and gained Him, according to the expression of an English exegetist, the "exercise of the dictation of the Spirit." From the evening of Easter we see the Lord Jesus Christ dispensing the Spirit and giving Him to His Church (John XX, 22). Henceforward we see Him become the "life-giving Spirit" (cf. Coloss. II, 9). He is impregnated by Him, He radiates Him. The Spirit will be for us not only the Spirit of the Father, or the Spirit of the Eternal Word, but also *the Spirit of the Risen Christ*.

The Christian: a body, a soul, the Holy Spirit

The Acts of the Apostles which have been entitled, with perfect truth, the Gospel of the Holy Spirit, reveal to us, from the moment of Pentecost, this pervading of the Church by the Holy Spirit.   Paul will address himself to Christians as being "spiritual."

It is again to St. Irenaeus that we owe that marvellous definition of the Christian as *"a body, a soul, the Holy Spirit."* At baptism those who have been reborn of water and the Holy Spirit have become a new race.   And the newness in them is the active presence of the Spirit of God, sent by the Father and the Son.   When the theology of the Middle Ages, so little disposed to be lavish with words, comes to pose the problem of discovering what is the soul of the community of Christians, it will be able to reply, without hesitation: it is that which unifies the Church as a living body surrounding the Risen Christ, that is, the Holy Spirit. The Mystical Body of the Lord would be better called, strictly speaking, His Spiritual Body (a Body animated by a Spirit).   There is in this a fundamental doctrine, happily brought to light again following upon the Encyclical *Mystici*

Corporis (1943), defining the Spirit as the soul of the Church. It is not possible to understand the life of the Church unless the most important place is given to the Holy Spirit.

The repercussions of these dogmatic findings upon moral theology may be divined.

II. A SPIRITUAL MORALITY

"Where love responds to love through the very dynamism of love itself, there is where perfect liberty blossoms. Grace and love totally unite the human will and the will of Christ in the Holy Spirit."[5] That is, of course, provided we do not close our hearts to the Spirit.

The Spirit is *our law;* our law, therefore, is a *law of love,* and consequently, a *law of perfect liberty.*

1. *The Law of the Christian, the Law of the Spirit*

The Christian, a person living in the sight of God, is placed under the direction of the Holy Spirit who is given to him in his own personal right from the time of his baptismal rebirth. The whole of his morality should consist in allowing the Spirit to well up within him.

The leaping fountain

To the question, who is the lawgiver of the New Testament, the reply, without any doubt is: Christ is the lawgiver

---

5. *La Loi du Christ* by B. Häring, I. "L'essence de la Loi nouvelle," p. 393.

of the New Testament. But one is thinking then of the Sermon on the Mount, and primarily of the precepts of our Lord. Now this is to misunderstand the newness of Christianity and to risk reducing it to the level of a pietistic and moralizing "revival." If Christ is the *lawgiver* of the New Testament, it is chiefly through the gift which He makes of the Holy Spirit, the leaping fountain of truth and of love, to the hearts of each and everyone of those who believe in Him. "If any man thirst, let him come to me, and drink. He that believeth in me . . . ." Now St. John points out, "this he said of the Spirit which they should receive, who believed in Him" (John VII, 37-39). The morality of the New Testament is the morality of the Holy Spirit which has become our law.

The new Sinai

Pentecost is the great manifestation of which Sinai was only the prefiguration. We recall how this feast of Pentecost was for the Jews not only a feast of the first fruits of the harvest but also a commemoration of *the giving of the law of the covenant on Sinai.*[6] It is certainly no mere chance that our Lord gave the gift of His Spirit to His followers on this very day of Pentecost. While on this particular day the first baptized were offered to God as the first fruits of the new humanity, on this particular day too the Spirit was given to the new people of God as His definitive law. *Pentecost,* in a most wonderful way, fulfills while going far beyond the promises of *Sinai.*

━━━━━━━━━━━━━━━━

6. Today, in modern Israel, Pentecost is still the feast of the giving of the Law.

The People of the Spirit

Through the grace of God the People of the Law became the People of the Spirit. The Israelites gladly called themselves the People of the Book (the Book par excellence, the Holy Bible). The Church before being the People of the Book is the People of the Holy Spirit. And there is certainly for us an indication of a fundamental spiritual attitude in this fact, that the liturgy allocates the greatest part of the Church's year *under the designation of Pentecost.* Those 25 or 27 Sundays after Pentecost teach us that the whole life of the Church—her pilgrimage towards the return of our Lord—is taking place under the direction of the Spirit of Christ, which has become her soul, her interior law and the law of each one of her faithful.

2. *The Law of the Spirit, a Law of Love*

A law of participation in the Holy Spirit

It is not enough just to say, the Spirit teaches and guides us. We must say, the Spirit "informs" us. St. Thomas, in fact, defines charity as the "form of the virtues;" "a certain participation in the Holy Spirit,"[7] *that is, in the Spirit of love.* "The charity of God is poured forth in our hearts, by the Holy Ghost who is given to us" (Rom. V, 5).

If, during His life on earth, the Son returned to the Father under the guidance of the Holy Spirit, this is, briefly, because it is eternally in the Spirit that He returns to the Father in the bosom of the Trinity. To say that He

----

7. IIa - IIae, q. 23 a, 3, ad. 3.

promulgates a law of charity is to say that He gives us a share in this *movement of the Spirit of love* in Him towards the Father.

A *law of trust and not of fear*

Christians do not have to make theirs the climate of fear which too often was the condition of Judaism under the Old Dispensation.[8]

The Spirit of Christ is, in us, *a filial spirit.* St. Paul, like St. John, insists upon this: he banishes the fear of the slave. "For you have not received the spirit of bondage again in fear; but you have received the spirit of adoption of sons, whereby we cry: Abba (Father). For the Spirit himself giveth testimony to our spirit, that we are the sons of God" (Rom. VIII, 15, 16). "Fear is not in charity: but perfect charity casteth out fear, because fear hath pain. And he that feareth, is not perfected in charity" (I John IV, 18).

One would be tempted to say that the Christian's spirit is by anticipation a spirit of quiet and rest, the Spirit by which the Son rests in the Father. No atmosphere is more favorable to growth.

----

8. Certainly one should not over-simplify in partisan fashion and allow it to be believed that love makes its appearance in Revelation only with the New Testament. The exegetists have high-lighted especially in the Judaism of the last centuries before Christ, amongst the "little ones of Yahweh," a delicacy which has nothing to envy in Christianity except the personal presence of our Lord and of the Holy Spirit. But it is undeniable that the Fathers of the Church, in seeking to characterize the evangelical life, have emphasized the change of atmosphere made possible by the Incarnation: henceforth life develops as a response of love to the God of love.

The law of restlessness and of folly

The law of quiet? This image should be corrected at once. We are not yet at the end of our road. *Irrequietum est cor nostrum* ... restless is our heart. We might have put it more aptly by calling it the law of restlessness. The Spirit cannot leave us at rest. He raises us tirelessly towards the Father. We do not expect that He will suggest quiet ways to us. He led Christ to Calvary. He is always linked with the Cross of Christ, with the folly of the Cross. "Now we have received not the spirit of this world, but the Spirit that is of God ... not in the learned words of human wisdom; but in the doctrine of the Spirit .... But the sensual man perceiveth not these things that are of the Spirit of God; for it is foolishness to him, and he cannot understand, because it is spiritually examined" (I Cor. II, 12-14). Nothing is more favorable to growth, did we say? But nothing is more demanding, either. Put simply, it is I who demand through love for another, or rather it is His Spirit become my own.

3. *The Law of Love, Law of Perfect Liberty*

We are at the heart of the Christian morality, at the heart of the great struggle led by St. Paul at the dawn of Christianity, when he wrote to the Galatians and to the Romans to shield them from the seduction of Judaism and a return to its practices, to its well-defined codes upon which one might calculate its justice. "Stand fast, and be not held again under the yoke of bondage" (Gal. V, 1). We do not wait for our justice from the law. "For we in spirit, by faith, wait for the hope of justice ... faith that worketh by charity" (Gal. V, 5-6). It is enough for us to live by the will of the

133

Spirit of Christ and we are free from all paralyzing bonds, free of the law.

Here we must quote Fr. Häring:

"The problem, or to express it more accurately, the mystery of Christian morality is that of a perfect interiorization of the law in respect of the essentially dialogical character of religion. The Christian does not govern his life upon a series of impersonal principles, but neither does he obey an ideal of perfection of himself. He obeys Another without, for all that, losing his ability to act freely according to his interior urge to the point of doing 'what he wants to do.' How is this possible?

"It is the mystery of our incorporation in Christ which resolves this antinomy and achieves this wonder. For the Christian obeys Christ, he follows Christ, but he is not condemned thereby to an external imitation—he lives in the Church, the Body of Christ, he possesses in himself the life of Christ, the *Spirit of Christ.* Thus he is able to respond with docility to God, while at the same time following his own interior principle, the Spirit of love, charity."[9]

Interior law, interiorized in love, the *law of liberty!* So, it is not a matter of an external gaze which petrifies us: it is a matter of a demand from free choice, coming entirely from within. It is for this response that Love thirsts, this is what Love desires to arouse in me.

The "god in us" according to the Greeks

Every man dreams of possessing *in himself* a profound inspiration and, as it were, the law of his own existence. Socrates spoke of his "demon," that *interior* divinity which

---

9. *La Loi du Christ* by B. Häring, III, p. 9.

dictated his conduct to him. And the pagans referred to this "god within us" who teaches us about good and evil.

Greek philosophy sounded the knell of the "interior demon" in favor of an impersonal natural law. A tremendous ... and a dangerous acquisition. For, pervading the world, the cosmos and humanity, this law rules the universe; but like any blind and implacable law without the intervention of liberty and the love of a living God. Hence the sage's ideal was that of an unresisting coincidence with the order of the world.

The "interior master" according to St. Augustine

The Fathers of the Church, bringing Christian doctrine face to face with the philosophic thought of their time saw the problem clearly. St. Augustine, in particular, endeavored to transpose the Stoic idea of the natural law, while firmly retaining the personalism of the Christian faith. We know, for instance, his commentaries upon the text of John XI, 28: "The master is come, and calleth for thee." At the heart of man, at the pinnacle of his spirit (*mens*) God speaks, enlightens and guides.... "Someone in me more myself than I" Claudel was to say, in most Augustinian language.

"The divine instinct" according to St. Thomas

St. Thomas, unlike many of his commentators, did not overlook this doctrine of the interior Master. We use the expression "interior" advisedly, and not simply invisible. At the center of the Christian existence St. Thomas places the *"mens"* or again, the *"affectus," the heart.* "The New Testament," he writes, "consists in the pouring out of the

135

Holy Spirit who teaches us from the interior.... Thus it is said, 'I will write my laws in their heart.'"[10] Everyone knows of these "intuitions" or "sentiments" which hardly ever are wrong; they do not derive from a demonstrable deduction but from a kind of mysterious instinct. St. Thomas considers that every Christian possesses thus a "divine instinct," along with the *gifts of the Holy Spirit,* and he applies to all those who live by it what Aristotle says only of the men of genius: "To those who are led by a divine instinct it is not desirable to give counsels according to human reason. Let them follow their interior instinct! A better principle than reason guides them."[11]

"I am free"

"Now the Lord is a Spirit. And where the Spirit of the Lord is, there is liberty" (II Cor. III, 17).

All holiness—and therefore all Christian morality—consists in doing the will of our Lord. But this is not a matter of some servile fulfillment. We must make our Lord's will our will. It must come about that His inspiration in us turns out to be the inspiration of our own wills. Then we are free. "I am free," says the sinner, and he is as enslaved as any one could possibly be—his liberty is captive, the captive of his passions, the captive of his sins. "I am a *prisoner of Christ,*" says St. Paul (Philem. 1), and *he is free* even in his chains, with all the joyous liberty of the Spirit.

Whoever submits to the imperatives of the Lord, to His Words, only under duress and not in His Spirit, "that man," says St. Thomas, "is still under the regime of sin, by which

10. *Comment. in Haebr.,* c. 8, 1-2.
11. IIa - IIae, q. 68, a. 1.

136

the will of man begins again to desire what is contrary to the law. Through grace this domination is broken so effectively that man fulfills the law not as a slave of the law but freely."[12] He genuinely bears the law in his heart: *Lex Dei in corde ipsius.*

The true roads of liberty

We know the supreme secret of this liberty of the children of God. It is the *miracle of love.* Love is the highest realization of my free individuality. And at the same time it fills me with raptures about the one whom I have chosen to love.

"The man who loves what God achieves in him and what God desires of him ... interiorizes all the laws, all the obligations, all the commandments. He loves what is asked of him and that coincidence of will and commandment, of desire and purpose, of love and duty, of the creature and the Creator is liberty itself: *Dilige et quod vis fac ...* love and do what you wish. Henceforth it is your only law .... And if anyone could love thus, in an absolute way, he would be absolutely free, because for him it would be one and the same thing to do what he wanted and to do what he should."[13]

St. Thérèse of the Child Jesus gives us an example of this in her simple and sublime confessions: "I never have any disappointments because I am always content with what God does. I desire only His will."[14] And again, "I let God choose for me. What He does is what I love."[15]

----

12. *Comment. in Rom.* c. 16, 1-3.
13. J. Mouroux, *Le sens chrétien de l'homme,* p. 159.
14. Quoted by A. Combes, *Introduction à la spiritualité de sainte Thérèse de l'Enfant-Jésus,* p. 287.
15. *Novissima Verba,* p. 19.

The true roads of liberty are the roads of love. Now, this love is something which God Himself implants in us. "God is poured forth in our hearts, by the Holy Spirit, who is given to us" (Rom. V, 5). Christian obedience is not some kind of passive carbon copy, a service imitation, a dreary conformity—it is the ready springing forth of the eternal love. It is the dynamism which relates Christ to the Father. The roads of liberty where Christ leads us are those of *divine liberty*—the only liberty, in sober truth, which has the power to flood our hearts, capable as they are of opening to the divine Love.

III. CATECHETICAL AND PASTORAL ORIENTATIONS

What is the place of the Holy Spirit and of His law in our catechetics or our pastoral work? Should we not be afraid that by over-emphasizing this theme we might be accused of illuminism and free thought?

A characteristic fact is that this theme of the law of the Spirit, so developed in the writings of St. Thomas, in the serenity of a faith removed from polemics, came to dwindle steadily with the passage of the centuries. In the 16th century it was no longer receiving practical discussion. Certain manuals on morality did not even allude to it. Yet we are faced with one of the most fundamental and original features of Christian morality, that is the morality of the Holy Spirit.[16]

▬▬▬▬▬▬▬▬

16. Cf. T. Maertens, *Le Saint Esprit dans la Morale*, (Fichier biblique), Bruges, 1960; J. Aubry, *Le Saint Esprit et notre vie spirituelle* (Ed. Fleurus), Paris 1956; A. M. Henry, *Le Saint Esprit* (coll. "Je sais, Je crois"), Paris 1961.

It is high time to control the last shudders of an obsidional fever by which we have been gripped through the Reformation and to recognize—without prejudice to a necessary obedience to the Church which we shall insist upon presently —the place which is being given again to the Holy Spirit in our pastoral work and our religious pedagogy, namely, the first place—always.[17]

We want to form good Christians—men of conscience, dutiful men, wise men. Are we really bringing up *men led by the Holy Spirit?*

Conscience and Spirit

We teach children readily, and from their earliest years, that they must follow their consciences, even when no one can see them, "because," we tell them, "God is everywhere and He sees you."

Nothing is truer, and yet there is a risk, which is not illusory, of inculcating in this way the kind of fear they might feel for a policeman. Let us teach them just as carefully that this voice of conscience, which is in all of them, is a voice of love, a call of love. Let us teach them to listen, in the happy phrase of St. Paulinus of Nola, to "the respiration of the Holy Spirit."

▬▬▬▬▬▬▬▬▬▬▬▬▬▬

17. This is not to say that the condemnations brought recently and justifiably against "the morality of the situation," which misunderstood the objectivity of the law and in particular of the natural law, should make us silent again, or shame-facedly minimize the role of the Holy Spirit in the Christian life. One cannot call upon the Holy Spirit in order to evade the Commandments; that is out of the question; but the person who stands by the letter of them so that he can confine himself to their minimal demands fulfills them badly. There is no true obedience to the Lord unless it is carried out in docility to the Spirit.

In the same way let us cultivate the practice of the examination of conscience. This is also the moment to go back to keeping one's ears open to the Holy Spirit, as St. Ignatius desired. Which are the calls of the Spirit we have heard and followed, which are those we have not wanted to hear and which remain unanswered? In the last analysis it is at each hour of the day, at each moment, that the Christian should hear, in the intimacy of his conscience, the murmur of the Spirit Who is saying to him: "Come to the Father."

Duty and Spirit

According to a suggestion of Père J. Tonneau, one should be able to distinguish two types of Christians, *the dutiful man and the spiritual man*.[18] One can discover them very easily in ecclesiastical and religious circles. Who does not know those pillars of observance, those punctual functionaries? They make for the solidity of an institution but in their attitude there is something stiff and cramped. They are so vigilant about never breaking through the guide-rails of duty that one might even say they need it in order to guide each step they take. If suddenly they find themselves in some unforeseen situation, something other than a "regular" situation, they are paralyzed and unable to take advantage of the opportunity it presents. The "spiritual men" also believe most certainly in rules and regular practices and in the wisdom embodied in them, but they are attentive first and foremost to the promptings of the Spirit. They have antennae for use in exceptional situations and for the occasions when they cannot see the way before them. They not only

18. D. S. A. M., t. III, art. Devoir, col. 660.

140

find the route but they sign-post it for others. The comple-
ments of those in the first category, how very precious are
these men in the Church of God!

Wisdom and the Spirit

We want—and rightly so!—*enlightened* Christians, and
hence we cannot give too much instruction provided, of
course, that everything is related to the promptings of the
interior Master and to His love. There are men who are
living books, learned, armed with notes, who have the
answer to everything. Impressive though they may be,
these men, unless their knowledge is interiorized, are as
much automatons as the books themselves. The divine
intention is not to make of us scholars of the moral sciences,
but beings who choose, who make up their minds and
personally involve themselves according to the Spirit of
Christ.

We desire *sensible Christians*. There are certain extrav-
agances which discredit religion. Nevertheless, even in
this age of conformity, we have to believe in the free
movements of the Holy Spirit and not fit ourselves too readily
to a standard morality. The Lord has humor and gladly
abandons our prefabricated frameworks. The Holy Spirit
is in charge of our Christian lives, and the fact is that He
does not work like a conveyor belt. In our great Catholic
family we are the brothers of the Fathers of the Desert,
reasonably eccentric, and of the extravagant stylites. The
charismatics have always had their place in the Church. In
the middle of the 19th century the Curé of Ars was a magnificent proof of this. What bishop of the period would have
classed poor Father Vianney as the leading parish priest in
all France?

We desire Christians who have the sense of the Spirit and who allow themselves to be guided by His divine instinct. Let us not then systematically reject all originality.

Christians in fact demand *reasonable solutions*. It is enough to think on the dramas of certain penitents. And God knows when the human and reasonable solution is emotionally tempting. Most frequently it is a betrayal of the evangelical spirit. May the Holy Spirit preserve us from confusing Christianity with a purely reasonable ideal! If our morality is a morality of the minimum resolutely adopted as a line of conduct, if, by dint of wanting to be intelligent, our moral intelligence becomes an exercise in casuistry which excuses everything, then we are wandering away from the Christian climate where the law of the Spirit holds sway. "For the foolishness of God is wiser than men" (I Cor. 1, 25).

Is there, in conclusion, any need to insist upon this? No one can call upon the Spirit in order to escape the objective demands of the law but only in order to pass them out on the way to better things. Liberty is not license. "He alone can claim the liberty of the children of God who has declared a total war 'upon the works of the flesh' and is ready to live 'by the Spirit,' by that Spirit Who brings us, with Himself— at once a newness of being and a new source of obligation— *the depths of His Liberty.*"[19] The only method of hearing His liberating call is to open oneself to Him in prayer. *Veni Sancte Spiritus!*

---

19. *La Loi du Christ* by B. Häring. I, p. 395.

CHAPTER SEVEN

THE LAW OF CHRIST, THE LAW OF THE CHURCH

The Spirit leads us to the Father by a sure route, by the
only route. But who can assure us that this is indeed the
voice of the Spirit of truth which we hear and not that of
the spirit of darkness and of lies. Is there not a risk at the
least, as Pastor Boegner expresses it so effectively, that "reason may take the place, among many people, of the inner
testimony of the Holy Spirit?"[1] Are we given over completely to interiority, without any control, without any
exterior objective rules? In placing the accent upon the
"interior master," have we not minimized that of order,
regularity and discipline?

Not at all. Why? Because the Spirit guides us according to the Word of Christ, and the Church acts as our interpreter.[2] In other words, He guides us *in the Church*. The
Christian route is a route of the Spirit, but it is also, by
reason of that very fact, a route of the Church. *To stress
the part played by the Spirit is to stress the part played by
the Church.*

To be convinced of this it is enough to submit oneself

---

1. *Qu'est-ce que l'Église?* by M. Boegner, 1931, p. 91; cf. p. 59: "In
many areas of reformed Christianity, *personal judgment* has taken the place
of the interior testimony of the Holy Spirit."

2. Cf. *La Loi du Christ* by B. Häring, t. 1, p. 362.

to the logic of the faith, as magnificent as it is rigorous: the law of the Christian is the law of Covenant, the Law of the New Covenant in the *Spirit of liberty*, and therefore the law of the People of the New Covenant, that is, *the Church*. Anyone who wishes to remain in contact with the Spirit and to let himself be guided by Him must remain in contact with the Church and let himself be guided by her; for it is to her, to the Church His Spouse, that Jesus gives His liberating Spirit.

But do we really believe that?

I. "I BELIEVE IN THE HOLY SPIRIT IN THE CHURCH"

1. *"Where the Church is, there is the Spirit of God."*

"I believe *in* the Holy Spirit *in* the Holy Catholic Church *for* the remission of sins, the resurrection of the body and life everlasting."[3] This formula with its precise interlocking of prepositions, is unusual. Yet it is not at all unlikely that this is the original formula of our Credo. It welds the Spirit to the Church for all times, just as, equally, it links the Church to the Spirit, the Spouse to the Spirit of her Spouse. Those who reject this link understand the Church no better than they understand the Spirit.

"The Holy Spirit *in* the Church:" how timely it would be to restore this formula! It seemed of use at the very beginning of Christianity because Illuminism was already

----

3. Cf. *Je crois à l'Esprit Saint dans la Sainte Église*... by P. Nautin, coll. "Unam Sanctam," 1947.

144

making its appearance then. But our era of social disorganization knows better than other epochs the temptations of prophetic anarchy. The proliferation of sects, of the Pentecostal type and sub-varieties, bears only too eloquent testimony to this.

But there must be a defense in depth here. There is no question of limiting the Spirit by the Church, unless this is in the sense whereby the body limits the soul but at the same time ensures its presence.

Or, rather, going beyond all defense reflexes, let us say positively that *we shall give back with assurance to the Spirit of Christ* His full place in our renewed morality *only if we simultaneously give Him His full place in the Church.*

Pentecost is bound up with the Church. It is the date of the Church's birth. Conceived on Calvary, the Church was born on Pentecost Day. Nothing should seem more obvious to us. It is the company gathered together on this day which visibly receives the Spirit. And this visible mission of the Spirit perpetuated in the visible Church is a mystery quite as important and real as the visible Incarnation. It is as the result of this, and by means of this that the Spirit of Christ will be communicated, and It will not be given outside of this. We know the saying of Ignatius of Antioch, who was completely convinced of the presence of the Holy Spirit in the hearts of the faithful: "Where the bishop appears, there let the people be, just as where Jesus Christ is, there is the Catholic Church,"[4] and the concise utterance of St. Irenaeus: "Where the Church is, there is the Spirit of God and where the Spirit of God is, there is the Church and all grace."[5]

---

4. *Letter to the Smyrnaeans,* 8, 2.
5. *Against the Heresies* III, 24, 1.

145

The conversion of St. Paul, staggering and spectacular, is surely the work of the Holy Spirit, acting, if one may be so bold as to put it that way, as a free-lance and on His own account. It is striking, on the other hand, to note that while the intervention of heaven closes the eyes of Saul to the false lights of this world, only the Church, in the person of Ananias and then of Peter, opens the eyes of Paul to the fullness of the faith. The Church is always there as a necessary witness of the Spirit.

The *Word of God* is addressed to all men. But it is found in the Bible and this *treasure is confided to the Church* not only to safeguard it but so that it may be given authentic interpretation. One might say that it devolves on the Church to utter herself the word which created her. The same paradox holds good for the sacraments, of whose importance in morality we shall speak later: they were entrusted by Christ to His Church; and while it is true that the sacraments of Christ make the Church, it is none the less indisputable that *it is the Church which makes the sacraments.*

2. The Church, "Milieu" of the Spirit of Christ

How should this role of the Church be conceived? Is she, then, the intermediary between the Spirit of Christ and us? Ought we to consider our faith as mediate? To the extent that we get further away from the Apostles and that we are dealing with the successors of their successors, ought it to be said that our faith is more and more mediate, *mediatissima?*

The "Vicaire savoyard" makes this protest:

"These are men who are going to tell me what God has said? I would much rather have heard God Himself; it would not have cost Him more and I should have been safe from the ever-present possibility of being led astray by human witnesses. Must there always be men who are relating to me what other men have related? What a lot of men between God and me!"[6]

In truth the dilemma of whether revelation is mediate or immediate must be rejected. Revelation is *formally immediate*: our act of faith, as equally our spirit of hope and our adherence to charity, touch God immediately; no one in this dialogue interposes between God and our hearts. We possess the testimony of God in us and according to the somewhat paradoxical text of St. John we "have no need that any man teach" us (I John II, 27), for, thanks to the Spirit of Pentecost who teaches us, we *not only learn* the truth but we *see* that God has spoken in Jesus Christ and that he has entrusted his word to the Church.

Conversely, Revelation is *materially mediate*. The Spirit teaches us from within to receive, from without, the teaching of Christ entrusted to this Church in which the Spirit is present. It is her concern to settle through her agreed faith the content of the faith of all. It is her concern to determine infallibly what must be believed. In order to communicate with the Spirit *we communicate with the Church*. The magisterium of the Pope and the bishops is the main agent of this determinative function. It is also the natural protector of the orthodoxy of the faith. To communicate with the Church *we obey the Hierarchy*.

It is as unthinkable, for a Christian, to appeal from a visible and hierarchical Church to a Church which is completely spiritual and invisible as it is to claim to go straight

---

6. *L'Émile ou de l'Éducation*, by J. J. Rousseau, 1, IV, Profession de foi du Vicaire savoyard, Geneva 1810, p. 56.

to God and to His Spirit without passing through Christ. This ecclesial mediation of the faith is the actual logic of the Incarnation. Through grace, through generosity, God becomes man to introduce us to his friendship. Prepared by a race of men, Israel, a prophetic race, the revelation of the Incarnate Word is logically transmitted through a race of men, the Church, a teaching society. But it would be much more suitable to speak, not of an intermediary between God and us, but of a *living milieu*. The Church is this living milieu where God calls us together, where His grace touches us, where His word is expounded, *the place necessary for our immediate encounter with God,* human indeed, but as little interposed between God and us as the Body of Christ.

II. AN ECCLESIAL MORALITY

Our morality is born of faith, therefore it is inseparable from the Church.

The philosopher's maxim is that we must live according to reason, while St. Paul's "just man liveth by faith" (Rom. I, 17). So the philosopher, when he seeks to detect the principles and the ways for his moral conduct has nothing else than his reason to consult: he passes judgment on the philosophic tradition itself. With all due deference to the "Vicaire savoyard" who would like to be thus on the plane of Revelation ("Apostle of truth, what have you to say to me, then, of which I do not remain the judge?"[7]), when the Christian seeks to discover the paths of his Christian life he does not have to consult his reason in the first place.

---

7. *Loc. cit.*

He can *leave the matter* (more or less consciously during the first years) *to the Church*: it is from her that he is learning to love as a Christian; she is truly for her sons the "educator of consciences." Everyone could repeat with Claudel: "Praised for ever be this great, majestic Mother at whose knees I have learnt everything."[8]

The natural law may remain as distinct as can be from positive precepts; it is itself caught up in the law of Christ, and therefore in the teaching of the Church.

The Christian cannot be a "brother of the free Spirit." In the course of centuries, sects of this nature have always blossomed. The Spirit, to be sure, teaches us liberty, but how could he involve us in a kind of anarchic liberalism, he Who is the node of the eternal communion? Our conscience is the voice of God, of the Spirit of God, only in so far as it remains in accordance with the voice of the Church. Any spirit who would withdraw him from the way outlined by the Church would be a lying one for the Christian.

"It is not, therefore, a matter of saying or thinking: I have my own conscience, so I am in line with the divine law . . . . We must say: my conscience, which is loyally informed, is in accord with the law of God and the teachings of the hierarchical Church; therefore I am in line and I act in consequence."[9]

We need not conclude from this that submission to the Church will stifle the Spirit but rather that the *Church should always remain*, through the fervor of all, a spiritual people. It is a well-known fact that the saints of the Church who have been the most eccentric and disconcerting have been the ones most devoted to communion with the Church.

---

8. *Ma conversion*, in *Contacts et circonstances*, by P. Claudel, p. 17.
9. Pastoral letter of Cardinal Feltin, on the Feast of All Saints, 1960.

According to the twofold richness of the mystery of the Church this ecclesial character of our morality will signify *community solidarity and hierarchical submission*, it being understood, of course, that the Hierarchy is at the service of the community but that the community has no stability here on earth outside of the hierarchical structure.

1. *A Morality of the Community Solidarity*

The sociologists have shown us (this has become a truism) the importance of social phenomena in the shaping of our individual behavior, in particular the influence exerted by their environment in life upon the thought and the customs of men. The sociological school goes even so far as to state, in respect to morality, that society is the unique source of moral sense.... To each environment its own morality; to happen to be set in a certain environment is to adopt its morality.... This is something which takes place, we readily agree, in the case of people who have not strong personalities. But we reject the *collectivist* misuse of this theory. Do we suspect *individualism* so much?

It is true that each one of us has his own personal route to follow and from that he cannot escape. This is not individualism so much as an affirmation of the primacy of the individual, provided that it is not forgotten that the individual himself is interpersonal, inescapably a tributary of the environment which he influences and by which he is influenced.

We cannot above all believe that the Holy Spirit makes an exception to this law. Our route along the "roads of (moral) liberty" is marked out by the *community conscience of the Church*, by the *sense of the faithful*. Even for the strongest personalities, this sense of the faithful is the *norm of morality* and no one may ignore, on behalf of his own personality, the influence to which he is subject and that which he himself exerts around him. As Congar puts it, recalling that "the Spirit is given to each one only in the communion of all," "He who is the principle of personalization of the faith and of the Christian life is given in a unified structure for a task of unification."[10] *This requisite attention to environment* must, moreover, have no hint of passive submission in it, but *conscious interaction,* and must in no way at all blur the duty of *personal affirmation.*

Attention to environment

Too often we concern ourselves with community environment and the collective conscience in a purely negative sense: namely, by care not to scandalize those around us. This is an elementary reflex. We ought to consider our place in the social structure in a more positive way. How can we make each and every one of our environments in life a focus of Christian living? Is it not, in the heart of the family, through seeing his parents living as Christians, that a child serves the most effective apprenticeship to his own Christian life? If school is so important it is because school too teaches us how to live, and the grave risk for Christian schools and colleges is that of being but a mediocre focus of Christian living. A living parish is an environment which educates in the faith, in prayer and in charity. As priests we are dependent, a great deal more than we think, on our sacerdotal environment, on its customs, on its mediocrity or its fervor. And finally we are, and we should be, open to the great movements of the universal Church . . . .

10. *Si vous êtes mes témoins,* by Y. M. Congar, 1958, pp. 32-34.

With regard to the community, to the nation, to all the environments of secular life, they also have had their influence upon us. A Christian owes it to himself continuously to improve his knowledge of these environments; it is not for him to follow in the wake of public opinion but to inform public opinion by discreet and continued activity, to strive to make the thought, the life and the charity of Christ shine out more radiantly in it.

The personal assertion

There is no reason why the fact of emphasizing the educative role of the community should lead us to underestimate the influence exerted in their own circles by *exemplary personalities*. Max Scheler has developed their preponderant role.[11] While the environment has its own importance, it definitely reflects and diffuses the influence of dominant personalities. Sociology analyzes from this point of view the function of leaders. Everyone knows that one or two pupils are sometimes sufficient to make or mar the atmosphere of a class and that a tiny coterie is sufficient to poison the climate of a parish. The personalist philosophers speak of the molders of consciences and their followers.

Outstanding personalities, leaders, molders of conscience exist also in the Church—they are the *saints*, whether canonized or not. These are the ones we must imitate. That means, first of all, that we must orientate ourselves about them: we must not copy them servilely, which would be the negation of the words of Our Lord according to which we have but one Master and that is Christ, but we must recognize plainly

---

11. *La Loi du Christ*, by B. Häring, t. III, L'apostolat de l'exemple, pp. 110-117.

that they help us to interpret the law of Christ and its demands at given periods. We must imitate them also by humbly but courageously accepting the fact that we may serve, we too, as models, by forging for ourselves personalities which will shine forth for that purpose. For priests it is a solemn duty: "Be ye followers of me," St. Paul makes so bold to say, (Phil. III, 17) and St. Peter exhorts his priests to be "made a pattern of the flock" (I Pet. V, 3).

2. A Morality of Hierarchical Submission

That the law of Christ is a law of the Church means also that it must be lived in communion with the Hierarchy, with its preaching and its sacraments.

The magisterium of Christian mores

When confronted by a Protestant who proclaims the primacy of the Word of God we all too easily feel uncomfortable and affected with an inferiority complex. A feeling of joy and of pride should rather animate us: for the Word of God, this bread which the Church breaks for us, is a *living* Word. With us too the rule of faith and of morality is the Word of God, but received in the living Tradition of the Church.[12] Is the Gospel therefore so easy to interpret on all its points?

It is not a precise code of law, it is a whole world, a whole revelation upon the mystery of God and the history of His covenant with us in Jesus Christ. In this domain all the words, even those of the Gospel, run the risk of being weakened. Where would some people not go, "given over"

----

12. *Council of Trent,* Denziger, 783.

to the Bible and to their individual conscience, without any real awareness of ecclesial community and without an undisputed magisterium upon faith and morality!

The Church, undoubtedly, will never dispense us from a personal search, but what support, what sustenance she supplies to us during this search!

Now, accustomed to refer to the magisterium for the determination of the truths to be believed, many of the faithful have no inkling that this magisterium enlightens also upon the truths to practice. We owe it obedience in that which concerns, according to the accepted formula, *faith and morals.*[13]

It is not necessarily a matter of infallible definitions. Will it not be thought some day that the greatest moralist of our times was Pope Pius XII? It is enough to consider the collection of his discourses or interventions to realize that he was able to face the most difficult moral problems of our period—that at a certain time he alone faced them—and that he delivered upon them judgments of sovereign balance.

What so often causes the magisterium of the Church to be forgotten in the matter of morality is that we so frequently reduce morality to the natural law alone and unconsciously withdraw this natural law from ecclesial government. Now this is an erroneous outlook—if the magisterium is responsible for the Gospel and for the positive divine law, it is also responsible for the correct interpretation of the

13. For an exposition, which is at once classic and full of nuances, of the degrees of this obedience, cf. *La Loi du Christ* by B. Häring, t. II. pp. 74-78.

natural law in so far as this latter is integrated with the evangelical law. The most recent popes have unceasingly reminded us of this and Jacques Maritain actually called Pius XII "the defender of the natural law."[14]

The sacramental life

The Word of God, in the Church, is inseparable from the *sacraments* and from the *liturgy*. Among the Fathers of the Church of the third and fourth centuries, as we have said, moral initiation took place ordinarily in the course of initiation into the mysteries and into the reception of the sacraments. In our day we have the tendency to reverse that order and to see the sacraments from the moral position as a "new field of duties"—the "duty" of Sunday Mass, the "duty" of annual confession or of the Paschal communion. To partake of the sacraments turns into "fulfilling one's religious duties." This is a detrimental attitude for the sacraments are not primarily "duties" added to other duties, they are gifts from God, the personal interventions of Christ in His Church, and these marvels of grace, these saving and sanctifying actions, are light for our Christian life itself. Our morality is sacramental, less because the sacraments mark out the stages of our Christian lives than because they illuminate our lives with a new light and confer a Christian "dynamism" upon them.

Now it cannot be forgotten that the sacramental life is unthinkable outside of the hierarchical communion. Even if Mass celebrated by an excommunicated priest is valid it has no meaning except in communion with the bishop.

---

14. *Documentation Catholique,* June 10, 1954, col. 422.

With regard to penance, it expressely assumes the jurisdiction of the Church.

Finally one may say that the Mass, where it welds together the *community of the faithful* under the *government of the Hierarchy,* is the fountain head, the living source of all our morality. It is there that the Spirit of Christ nourishes His Church.

III. CATECHETICAL AND PASTORAL ORIENTATIONS

The most specific application which can be made of this doctrine is obviously that of the spiritual direction given *in the name of the Church.* This is of interest not only to priests but also to educators and those whom they direct.

Spiritual paternity

The function of the spiritual father has always been an important charism in the Church. The early Eastern Christians held him in great reverence even before the practice of private penance was made general.[15] The very name "abbé" means "father." And the capital part played by the Abbé Huvelin in the life of Father de Foucauld should be recalled. It was he who oriented him and thus allowed him to make his life a journey of permanent fidelity to the Holy Spirit.

Now today it can happen that the administration of the Sacrament of Penance to people one after another may give a wrong emphasis to a priest's work and reduce to a

----

15. *Direction spirituelle en Orient, autrefois,* by I. Haussherr, Rome, 1955.

poor level his ministry of spiritual fatherhood; men pressed for time and overworked "distribute" in some haste a few moral counsels or some remedies, but they do not have time any more to be true spiritual fathers.

"The director of souls, the confessor, is more, or should be more than the simple moral theologian with some experience of life. It is true that he should be a moral theologian, for with good will one may learn this science and, generally speaking, God does not come to the aid of our laziness or our ignorance with any celestial charisms. But he should, properly speaking, be something more—a comrade-in-arms to obtain heavenly enlightenment, a worshipper who pleads, along with his disciple, for the knowledge of God's will and who does not imagine that he always knows it simply because he has in fact learnt moral theology. He should be the agent who reacts in a more sensitive way to the divine solicitations; he should have the courage to carry, together with him who is in his charge, the burden of the decision: in short, he should really be an enlightened spiritual father which, indeed, one does not become by pretending to be one."[16]

The Law of the Church, Law of Liberty

As he is the representative of the Church the spiritual father should unwearyingly kindle in hearts the meaning of the Church and love for her laws. To inculcate respect for institution, authority, discipline, order, law and regularity in the Church is his work.[17]

――――――――――――――――

16. *Dangers dans le catholicisme d'aujourd'hui* by Karl Rahner, Paris 1959, p. 51.

17. The "Rules of Orthodoxy" from the Exercises of St. Ignatius which were composed when confronting Protestantism should be re-written for

"It would be necessary, I think, to submit me to torture for a long time before wrenching from me one word against Canon Law itself."[18] We would do well to make our own, without hypocrisy, these words of Y. M. Congar! And equally, in those hours when we have to suffer from the representatives of the Church, this prayer of Newman to his Creator:

"May I not forget for an instant that you have established on earth a kingdom which belongs to you, that the Church is your own work, your establishment, your instrument, that we are under your guidance, your laws and your gaze—that when the Church speaks it is you who are speaking. May familiarity with this wonderful truth never make me insensitive—may the weakness of your human representative not lead me to forget that it is you who are speaking and acting in them."[19]

But the establishment within the Church is always at the service of the Spirit. Every pastor should therefore take pattern from the prudence of the Law: no more orders than are necessary to promote a true spiritual service; no superstitious support for ancient regulations which are no longer relevant; a constant care to promote an obedience which is not servile but "spiritual," that is to say, which is directed to the Holy Spirit through His witnesses and agents.

The spiritual father should remember—and should remind people—that the Church does not have to give us, and we should not expect from her, prefabricated standards of morality right down to the tiniest details. There is a

our times. Cf. especially No. 13: ". . . credendo inter CHRISTUM Dominum nostrum, Sponsum, et Ecclesiam ejus Sponsam, eumdem esse Spiritum, qui nos gubernat et regit ad salutem animarum nostrarum."

18. *Si vous êtes mes témoins,* by Y. M. Congar, p. 49.

19. Quoted in Newman by L. Bouyer, p. 428.

whole field for personal initiative and liberty of maneuver which the Church respects. To renounce this, under the pretext of a greater fidelity would be infantilism. St. Francis de Sales said once that it was doing a bad service to the Apostolic See to be constantly hanging on to its doorbell in order to ask for orders.[20] This would need to be repeated today, for the sake of certain souls who would have the inclination to consider flight from their responsibilities as a higher form of submission to the Church.

To sum up, for supreme victory over legalism, but also supreme fidelity to the Church, a spiritual society, one should disturb souls who are readily content with a reassuring ecclesial conformism: the boat of Peter, outside of which there is no salvation, is not a pleasure boat upon which one can settle down to sleep in complete quiet. According to Newman's celebrated saying, *to be at ease is to be unsafe.* Let us translate that here in this way: to be in conformity with the rules is not necessarily to be in a state of security. I am in conformity with the law; but am I in conformity with the Holy Spirit? Does He not formally ask *more* of me? We must have the courage and the lucidity to place the problem in this perspective: for the law is not a safeguard in itself (any more than was the Temple for the Israelites in the time of Jeremiah); the law is at the service of the Holy Spirit and its standards leave a sufficiently large field for spiritual liberty.

----

20. Quoted by Dom Lambert Beauduin, *La Maison Dieu.* 1945, No. 1, pp. 16 et seq.

CHAPTER EIGHT

THE LAW OF CHRIST, THE LAW OF LOVE

The Christian, having entered the Community, guided by the Spirit and the Church, now sees his life developing as a part of history made holy.

What is the motive power of this history, what is the dynamism which carries it forward, and towards what end is it being carried? What, in fact, is being made?

For a Marxist, the motive power of history is the class struggle for the abolition of class and the advent of a new man—fraternal man, to be precise. It is a grandiose concept. A Christian concept gone mad and cruel. It is a concept which has crushed, and will crush, generations of mankind. It is a concept which reaches out towards love by means of hatred, and naturally the love towards which it reaches is stunted and illusory.

"Hatred of the enemies of the Soviet people, of the Soviet Fatherland and of human progress is an indispensable characteristic of socialist humanism. In so far as these enemies exist, in so far as they act openly or clandestinely, it is the intensity of the hatred felt for them which constitutes in a man the measure of his love and his regard for those who labor and fight for the happiness of the people .... The Communist ethic sets forth against the

161

hypocritical commandment of Christian morality, 'Love your enemies,' a commandment to hate the enemy."[1]

"The humanism of the proletariat demands an implacable hatred of the petits bourgeois, of the power of capitalism, of capitalist values, of the parasites, fascists, tormentors and betrayers of the working class, a hatred of everything which causes it to suffer and of all those who live on the sufferings of hundreds of millions of men."[2]

For a Christian, humanity is involved in an immense adventure, namely, the gathering of all mankind in Jesus Christ, the progressive construction of the Mystical Body which grows towards its completion by uniting human individuals through love. It is not hatred which will overcome the division, which will consume the evil—it can only be love, *the fire of charity.*

Diego Fabbri, echoing St. John (XVII, 21-23) and the second chapter of Isaiah, is not wrong in appealing to the *Sign of Fire,* and of attributing to St. Ignatius (*ignis*) his cry of "El Fuego."

"Love! Call upon the Crusade of Love, everything else can fall into ruins, sink into nothingness. Set fire to this flame, your sign will be recognized and whole peoples will set out towards it . . . . Towards the Fire!"[3]

In its apotheosis, the Most Holy Trinity, and in its principle, the Spirit of Christ, Sacred History is a history of love.

---

1. A. F. Chichkine "Osnovy Kommounistitches Koy morali," *Fondements de la morale communiste.* Moscow 1955 pp. 242 et seq.

2. Maxim Gorki, quoted and approved by E. D. Modrjinskaia, *Contre les falsificateurs bourgeois du marxisme,* Moscow 1958, pp. 64-65; translations in E. Delimars, *Réfutation soviètique de quelques doctrines de philosophie et d'éthique de l'Occident.*

3. Diego Fabbri, *Le Signe du Feu,* l'Avant-scène, Feb. 1. 1961, p. 30.

This truth of *faith* is inscribed in the mystery of the Church (I). This mystery consequently defines not only the framework of our *morality* but its tenor and its very essence (II). We must live, and we must, as *pastors or catechists,* make others live the communion of saints (III).

I. THE CHURCH, IMAGE OF AND PARTICIPATION IN THE LIFE OF THE TRINITY

"A single heart, a single soul"

From its very origins, verifying the commandment and the promise of the Lord, the Church has appeared as an intimate united group, a community in which there was "but one heart and one soul" (Acts IV, 32). Should we not indeed look back with nostalgia upon that primitive Church of Jerusalem whose family atmosphere is so keenly evoked by St. Luke (Acts II, 42-47; IV, 32-35). Even after the Church has expanded throughout the wide world, to love one's brethren will remain a distinctive sign of the Christian and make him different from the pagans who are without heart, "without affection" (Rom. I, 31; II Tim. III, 3). For St. Ignatius of Antioch the Church is an *Agape,* and he unwearyingly exhorts: "... come together all of you with undivided heart."[4]

What is the basic reason for this new community? It is faith in the risen Christ, renaissance in the Holy Spirit. The Christian loves his brethren because he loves his God. He imitates his God in loving his brethren, this God who through love gave His Son to men, this God who is Jesus

---

4. *To the Philadelphians,* 6, 2; *To the Romans,* the salutation.

Christ has loved them unto death. The faithful, in return, moved by the same love which propelled God towards men, are carried along towards one another. In the eyes of all, the life of Christ appears as a *love of the Father*, but a love embodied in and made visible through a *love of men*. "Love one another as I have loved you," said our Lord; love one another with the same love as I have loved you, which is with the same love as I love my Father.

Here then is a fact: on the one hand, primacy is accorded in the Church to love of one's fellow man, a primacy such as is not encountered to the same degree in any other religion; a primacy so essential that to doubt it is to renege from the true Christian spirit. On the other hand, the presence of the love of the Father in Jesus Christ is, as it were, the sole explanation of such fraternal love. So love of men and love of God is mutually involved.

The idea of the person

At the heart of the *Trinity* God exists as Father, Son and Holy Spirit only in an eternal interpenetration of recognition, of love and of personal communion. Each divine Person possesses himself infinitely because he gives himself to the others infinitely so as to exist only as a "subsisting altruism" (M. Zundel).

Man, the image of God, realizes himself by imitating the divine Persons in this life of personal reception and gift. Christian theologians, for whom the mystery of the Incarnation threw light upon the individual as an autonomous person with freedom of choice, have now found in the mystery of the Holy Trinity a new light upon the *human person*. If the human person is a personal center which is established in itself, it is so established only in *relation to*

164

others, seeking them out in order to recognize them in a movement of love and respect, of reception and gift. We should speak even of an originating solidarity, interior to our taking up of a free position which nevertheless demands it. Our liberty will have to be part of this solidarity in order either to disown or to ratify it. In every way "I am myself only in so far as I open myself to others; I communicate only with myself to the extent that I communicate with others."[5] "To be deprived of others is to be deprived of self."[6] The concept of subject is essentially the concept of a society of subjects.

Sin and Salvation

In the eyes of Christian tradition sin is a breach of man's communion with God and a setback to the communion of men with one another. The Fathers have handed down from one to the other the simile of humanity considered as a huge mirror of God which, as the result of sin, fell to earth and shattered into pieces. Breaking their vertical link with God, human individuals break their horizontal link with one another: they have ceased then to be the image of the Trinitarian communion. Salvation will be the re-establishment, through Christ, of the communication of men with God and of men with one another. St. Paul speaks (Eph. II, 14) of the wall of hatred which Christ has come to break down between men, Jews and pagans, types of the whole of mankind, by reconciling all of them with God. St. John, in his turn, is to say that Christ died "to gather together

5. G. Marcel, *Du refus à l'invocation,* p. 50.
6. G. Gusdorf, *Traité de Métaphysique,* p. 279.

in one the children of God that were dispersed" (John XI, 52). Through His Cross Christ assumed a Mystical Body where men gathered in Him meet one with another and find at last their true being.

"One like Us, one in Us"

Such is the mystery of the Church, in the image of the Trinity, or better, in the Trinity. For if human beings are thus reunited with one another in Christ this is because the Holy Spirit, the link of love between the Father and the Son, is communicated to men through the risen Christ. "That they may be *one as we also are one*" (John XVII, 11 and 22): thus is the fraternal communion upon earth presented as an image of the communion of the Trinity. And Christ indicates the profound source of this unity: "I in them, and thou in me" (John XVII, 23). It is because the union of man takes place in Christ that it is realized not only in the image of the Trinity but in the Trinity: "one in us" (John XVII, 21).

The Holy Spirit is communicated to Christians in their Baptism and through the sacramental life which radiates around the Eucharist. Thus endowed, they can live their communion with God and at the same time their fraternal communion. The Father and the Son possess each other totally because they give themselves to each other in the Holy Spirit; in the same way, human individuals, thanks to this same Spirit, are all the more themselves in that they give themselves more to one another, all the more perfectly themselves in that they are, one with another, "perfectly one" (John XVII, 23).

II. A MORALITY OF CHARITY

Love of God or love of neighbor?

This mystery of the Church defines our morality for us: it is necessary to love; and it places it at once above the dilemmas with which jurists of all ages have concerned themselves: Whom is it necessary to love? God or man?

"... A doctor of the law asked him, tempting him: Master, which is the great commandment in the law? Jesus said to him: Thou shalt love the Lord thy God with thy whole heart, and with thy whole soul, and with thy whole mind. This is the greatest and the first commandment. And the second is like to this: Thou shalt love thy neighbor as thyself. On these two commandments dependeth the whole law and the prophets" (Matt. XXII, 35-40).

This is a "similitude" upon which we ought to meditate unceasingly. We should compare the "whole law" of this text with that of St. Paul who seems even to reduce "the Law in its fullness" to the second commandment: "For he that loveth his neighbor, hath fulfilled the Law" (Rom. XIII, 8, cf. 10), going so far as to state categorically: "For all the law is fulfilled in one word: Thou shalt love thy neighbor as thyself" (Gal. V, 14). We should revolve constantly in our minds the texts of St. John which bring us back from the love of God to the love of our brethren: "If any man say, I love God, and hateth his brother, he is a liar" (I John IV, 20), and from the love of our brethren to the love of God: "In this we know that we love the children of God: when we love God and keep his commandments" (I John V, 2). But in fact, what is He commanding us? To love our brethren! (I John IV, 21). Is this not *the* commandment of our Lord? (John XV, 17 ...).

Should it be said that nothing is simpler? Or that nothing is more mysterious? Would love of one's neighbor triumph in practice? And what becomes of self-love so well represented by the proverb, True charity begins at home?

The two principles

After so many recent works on Christian sources—"A reading of the balance sheet of historical and scriptural researches results in one over-riding impression, and that is the *predominance* accorded, *almost unanimously*, to the *problem of charity*"[7]—no one any longer contests "the existence of a primacy of charity in the moral life of the Christian."[8] But we are a long way from resolving all the questions through this agreement:

"The morality of charity which expresses the traditional essence of the Christian revelation is in fact so simple to understand in its popular and non-technical formulation, summed up by the Gospel and by St. Paul, that it is a delicate task to formulate all its moral articulations technically."[9]

We think that primarily it is essential to hold firmly to the two following principles:

1) *Charity towards God and charity towards our neighbor are mutually involved through grace.* If the latter is like the *sacrament* of the former it is because it derives its authentic principle in the former: it is *divine*.

2) *Charity towards one's neighbor and charity towards*

7. Ph. Delhaye, *L'Ami du clergé*, No. 68 (1958), p. 23.

8. R. Carpentier, *Le primat de l'amour dans la vie morale*, in N. R. T., No. 83 (1961) p. 4.

9. G. Gilleman, *Morale chrétienne en notre temps*, in *Lumière et Vie*, No. 50 (1960), p. 70.

oneself are connaturally inseparable. The second lives on the first for authentic love of self is *oblative* or it is not authentic.

Of such are the depths of the mystery of the Church and of our morality.

1. *Unification of the Love of God and the Love of Men*

It is always difficult to realize into what a network of personal relations we are introduced when we become a part of the people of God:

The love of God includes love of men

Whoever loves the Father loves Christ.

The One with whom we first of all communicate is God. Charity poured out in our hearts by the Spirit carries us towards *the Father* in Jesus, for this Spirit is the Spirit of the Son who said "Father" (Rom. VIII, 15); but we cannot love the Father without loving *His Son* towards whom the Spirit, the bond of their communion of love, eternally carries him.

Whoever loves Christ loves all men.

Now, to love the Son with the Father is to love him as he is—the risen Christ, indissociable henceforth not only from his physical body but from his Mystical Body, from all men saved by Him, "ordained at least to the Mystical Body" (*Mystici corporis*). This is a whole world of people from whom he does not wish to be separated any more. To emphasize "the eminent dignity of the poor in the Church,"

169

Bossuet presented them as "our Lord's poor," and "Jesus Christ suffering in the immensity of the poor." An even more daring formula of the Middle Ages referred to "Our Lord, the poor." We ought to go further still. Our Lord assures us, "to love me it is necessary to love my brethren, all men, who are me;" lest we fail to have a true personal communion with the living God we must love all men.

The love of men includes the love of God

If the love of God in the charity of the Holy Spirit shows us that we must not reject communion with a single human individual, the love of men, in its turn, in this same charity, opens us up to communion with God.

Whoever loves his brother loves Christ.

To love man truly it is necessary to meet him not in the opaque density of an object, as some thing in front of me which is getting in my way, but in a profound subjectivity. For this converts him into an "I," a person with whom we are in dialogue. This places him in a state of unique reciprocity with all men, his brothers, who can address him as "you" and unite themselves with him in the "we" of a community which will be the outcome of their solidarity. I cannot meet this man, cannot truly respect his uniqueness as an individual, unless I consider him as "a collegial reality,"[10] unless I want to love him for his own sake, without the others.

It is said "lovers are alone in the world." However that

10. M. Nédoncelle, *La réciprocité des consciences*, p. 58.

may be one might reply, in one sense, lovers do not yet love each other—they are seeking a love whose fullness they will not understand until later on. But one can also say that they are isolated from the anonymity of the *crowd*. Love will bring them into the *community*. *I cannot love my brother without loving all men.* But then, whoever loves his brother loves Christ, for He alone in the world of sin in which we are, divine center of innocence, gathers all men, reconciles them, re-establishes that communication between them to which their being aspires. He alone makes of all men one single vine, one great tree.

Whoever loves his brother in Christ loves God.

This encounter is not solely human but also theological. It is so perhaps implicitly, but it really is so.

Some day or another, in fact, experiencing and studying the subjectivity of the human person must lead us to another capital discovery, which is that every individual, this "I" or this "you," is an ontological relationship with this other "You" par excellence, the supreme "You" of the Father of our Lord Jesus Christ, with whom our encounter, through grace, is for each and every one of us the most indispensable because it is the most personalizing.

"There are many souls," said Paul Claudel, "but there is not a single one of them with whom I am not in communion when it utters 'Our Father.'"[11]

All genuine love may appropriate to itself Dante's phrase: "I gazed at Beatrice and Beatrice gazed at God." Even if the other person, the human partner, does not consciously

----

11. P. Claudel, *Conversations dans le Loir-et-Cher*, cantique de Palmyre, p. 119.

171

gaze at God, even if he ignores God to the point of denying him, despite everything, in the depths of his personality, which does not depend on him for its existence, he is gazing at God. For he is a human personal subject, created in the image of God, for communion with God. He is searching for God, and his confrontation with him will put the final seal upon his individuality and upon his destiny. To love the other person truly is to love God at least obscurely. *"Ubi caritas et amor, Deus ibi est."*

The more we are loved the more we ought to make our own the confession Claudel puts into the mouth of the woman: "I am the promise which cannot be kept,"[12] unless God comes to the rescue. The wonder of this being whom we want to love passionately is that of being in reality this "you" indissolubly linked to God and to love him properly I must love God. Wherever there is a true personal encounter in a love without egoism, God is near. To let oneself be caught in the game of love for others (that divine trap) is one day or another to let oneself be caught in the game of a love for God which demands expression.

"I was sick and you visited me . . . ." (Matt. XXV, 36). "You have seen your brother, you have seen your God"[13] even if you did recognize him and if he waits until your death to show you his unveiled countenance.

2. *Unifying Love of Self and Love of Others*

The charity of the Holy Spirit allows to flourish without opposition the inclination which moves us towards God, as also that which moves us towards human beings. Does

12. P. Claudel, *La Ville*, 2nd version, finale.
13. *Logion of the Lord*, collected by Clement of Alexandria.

it also allow resolving in the same unity the duality of *love of self* and *love of others?* Or should we indeed stop at the dictum which legitimizes so many egoisms: "True charity begins at home?" By and large a loyal Christian feels reasonably uncomfortable when he invokes that maxim, considering that he has the example of the saints who endeavor primarily to love others, and the example of Christ above all who has loved us by totally forgetting himself.

Charity and logic

Charity provides the key to the radical unity between love of self and love of others. A human individual does not in fact begin by existing all alone, and subsequently by being placed in relationship with others. The inter-subjectivity of individuals goes back to their first instant: as soon as I exist I exist in relationship and reciprocity. I cannot begin by loving myself today so that this may put me in a position to love others tomorrow. The living logic of the individual induces me to live as a rational being, to ratify and to expand the original links which have been forged from me to others and from others to me.

My sinful liberty could undoubtedly choose the rejection of an egotistic isolation. But in fact to choose thus is to choose the suicide and suffocation of the human person.

Our propensity as individuals, under the charity of Christ, is to move towards others, those others whom the same grace turns towards us, through the often misunderstood depths of their being. Because we call to each other from the depth of our being and need each other to exist, I do not possess myself except in receiving the other, who in his turn only fulfills himself in receiving me.

The example of the Saints

All Christian experience, the lives of all the saints, establish this as a certain fact: the more anyone deepens in charity, the more he comes to the point of taking others very seriously and becomes obsessed to the point where he seems to attach no further importance to anything but others.

"There is no man more remote from the pre-occupations of the ego than the saint: he is not present to himself, except through his presence to other individuals and to God." [14] The saints seem to attach less and less importance to themselves and more and more importance to others. In Christ they experience, to an ever stronger degree, that solidarity which unites the members of Christ to one another. They take others earnestly and, in fact, take over responsibility for them. They truly support the weight of others, as if it were only others who counted, quite forgetting themselves.

And paradoxically, it is by acting in this way that the saints truly love themselves! There is no love of self which can isolate itself from love of others: this is a question of life or death. By giving themselves to others and forgetting themselves, the saints love themselves with the only true love—losing their selfish ego, constricted and limited, they find an "I" open to all the riches of other people and of God. The saints thus produce for us the unanimous proof that in Christianity one loves others not less than self, nor with an equal love, but in fact more than self, and that it

14. L. Lavelle, *Quatre saints*, p. 29-30.

is necessary to involve oneself quite as seriously in the salvation of others as in one's own. But at the same time they prove that this loftier way of playing the game of love of others represents in the climate of the Gospels the only true way to love oneself. Love of self and love of others are, in fact, only one single love, thanks to the charity of Christ.

III. CATECHETICAL AND PASTORAL ORIENTATIONS

The extensions of this teaching would be infinite. What is charity? Who is my neighbor? Et cetera. But what can we say about the pastoral or catechetical applications of it?

"The greatest of sins"

To begin with, we priests should take seriously the reproach addressed to us by Diego Fabbri through the mouth of his Jesuit, Hudson, in the *Signe du Feu*:

The girl: It is wonderful to hear priests speak of love.

Hudson: We are afraid of love, *we who should be the first to speak about it*. We who invented love.

The girl: You? Then how did you come to let this love be taken from you, let it be stolen by others? What a sin you have committed! What a sin!

Hudson: The greatest of sins. For it was he, the Crucified, who created Love....[15]

----

15. Diego Fabbri, *op cit.*, p. 25.

The law of Christ is a law of love. Fellow priests, are we yet preaching the love of God, the "Practice of Love of Jesus Christ," [16] with this very word, love? Are the famous "hesitations" of Lacordaire before "this name which has been too profaned" still current? .... ("Shall I utter the name of it? And why should I not utter it?" But it yet takes four more phrases before he dares to do so! "God Himself is love." Of course, this was just the skillfull use of suspense on the part of a natural orator whom this word in no way dismayed) .... It is quite true that we, too, "profane" it often through our own insipidity. The fire of charity should truly consume us. The love of Christ for His Father, should so strengthen us that we might dare to cry out our "Let us love one another" in the face of all the passions of the world which mock it.

Hudson: .... I tell you that we alone, yes, we, look at us fully face to face, *we know what Love is*. [17]

Our technological civilization, obsessed by "things," has more need than any other for someone to speak to it of love and the world of individuals. If the priest, or anyone who has the responsibility of transmitting the Christian message, has not the courage to reveal to human love his own lofty secret and that he is the son of eternal love, then who will dare to do so? Once more we might recall, with the same Lacordaire:

"This is not a thing to talk about; it is necessary to shed

16. St. Alphonsus Liguori.
17. Diego Fabbri, *op. cit.*, p. 24.

blood over these words and thus confirm what has been said for God."

The sacerdotal mediation

The classic quarrel between theologians is whether the priesthood be defined by mediation or by sacrifice? Let us reply, without rejecting anything, that it must be defined through the *mediation of the Christian encounter*, of which the essential act in Jesus Christ is sacrifice.

All love is of a sacrificial order, for all love is oblation. It is not for nothing that the Mass, the sacrifice of Christ, is also the communion, the gathering of the Christian people, the encounter in the Body of the Lord of all the faithful forming the Mystical Body. The parish Mass is the sacerdotal and pastoral activity par excellence. All the rest is arranged in terms of that, all the fabric of the sacramental, educational, apostolic or mutually helpful mediations, which lead the priest to the heart of the community. We shall find them later as the concrete ramifications of morality and of pastoral activity.

Let it be enough to emphasize here (as a consequence of the *first principle*: the mutual involvement of charity towards God and of charity towards one's neighbor) that no pastor will ever be satisfied with having apparently established contact between his faithful and God by an assiduous practice of the forms of worship, if this charity towards God is not translated into a life of effective fraternal charity. On the other hand, no awakener of fraternal love in life can consider himself to have reached the end of his task except in so far as this charity has explicitly recognized its source, the Father, who has loved us so much as to give us his Son in the Sacrifice of the Cross offered at the Table.

177

Individual or Collective Formation?

The second principle, the reciprocal inclusion of love of self and love of neighbor, must not lead to superficial pedagogical applications. The current method in specialized Catholic Action cannot be universally imposed without nuances: formation through action and for action, that is to say, for and through the encounter with others from the point of view of natural encounters. Or rather, this providential method, which corresponds so well to what we have been saying of the "collegial" character of the personality, in no way excludes *individual formation.* Henri Marrou denounces it with too much acrimony when he writes, by way of contrast:

"In the far-off days of our youth the Church of France seemed less disturbed by the dechristianization of the masses than by the apostasy of the élites. One found wise and holy religious ready to concern themselves with the formation of one *single* pupil or one student; nobody was in any hurry then to become a 'militant,' responsible for a certain section of the apostolate; before sending anyone to evangelize his milieu, one was concerned first of all to ensure that he escaped the fate of a Lamennais, a Renan, a Loisy. The young Christians learned to know their faith."[18]

Let us state simply that this knowledge might have been full of pride and vanity if it had not been turned to knowing how *to love.* But let us confess that silent and loving formation is already *an encounter with others* whom one is preparing to serve better.

▪▪▪▪▪▪▪▪▪▪▪▪▪▪▪

18. H. Marrou, *Un homme dans l'Église,* special no. of *Esprit,* December 1950, p. 890.

It is thus for the priest himself. When he leaves the church after the celebration of his Mass, the priest, the first convert of his sacrifice, should be in *a state of encounter.* Open to all, his heart steeped in the charity of Christ, he will seek effective contact with his people, for the Good Shepherd effectively knows his sheep, he meets them. Therein is his being, his life. We make bold to state that a parish priest who, without valid reasons, does not visit his parishioners is in a state of grave fault.

But, on the other hand, what of the parish priest who is always running here and there without any thought for personal formation? Does he love sufficiently those he meets? Assuredly no, since he is offering them but a mediocre and negligent pastor, one with a narrow or old-fashioned kind of wisdom, uncertain solutions or ill-adapted advice. He must cultivate himself for *others.* This is, in any event, the only valuable culture. Every Christian educator should make this lesson his own.

Let us extend the conclusion. Our *examinations of conscience* are often tripartite—duties towards God, towards our neighbors, towards ourselves. Let us not fail to gather them in the unity of personal charity. To be sure it is I whom it concerns, with *my* duties. But "no man is an island," I exist only through and for others, in an oblative reciprocity which is the very essence of the spirit. The specified duties towards myself should not therefore cause me to fall into a morality of perfection of self for self, which would be the negation of a dialogical morality of charity towards God and towards others; I cannot live in a dialogue of love without seeing it transform my life and transform me myself. That is sufficient. Charity towards God and towards my neighbor asks nothing else of me, but that includes everything.

IV. AWAITING THE PAROUSIA

In order to hasten the supreme Manifestation of Our Lord (II Pet. III, 12) our daily task is concerned with His Epiphany here on earth.

A sacerdotal people, inspired by love, we make our earthly world show forth His glory by *an interior and visible* worship. We celebrate our Eucharist of Christ. Our desire is that this be ever more universal and ever more true until that time when He will return to transfigure our worship into a celestial liturgy (chap. IX).

This glory of God is thus given precise expression by man here on earth; worship brings home to us the realism of charity in our lives. We wish charity to be ever more penetrating and more active. We wish it always to reveal more clearly to us, and always to animate more deeply, the various demands of justice. Until the time when Christ shall come to transfigure our body of sin and wretchedness into His Body of glory and therefore finally to assimilate our human relations into the Trinitarian relationship (Chap. X).

CHAPTER NINE

THE LAW OF CHRIST AND WORSHIP

If the law of Christ is centered wholly and entirely upon a response of love, how does this love succeed in governing the whole of day-to-day living? What kind of living does it produce?

Will it produce a type of life governed by the cardinal virtues? Yes, it certainly will do that. Prudence, justice, fortitude and temperance are a quartet of virtues of Stoic origin which did not captivate the thought of the Middle Ages only. They intrigued Péguy sufficiently for him to sing of them in his quatrains, though not without delicately noting a certain hierarchy in them:

> O Cardinal Virtues
> of Pagan birth
> By Master and Prince received,
> Give way to your
> Theological Sisters
> Who were in Christ conceived.[1]

Were we, however, to allocate a place to worship within this compact format we should—though at the risk of a dessicated and juridical conception—have to base it on the virtue of justice.

▄▄▄▄▄▄▄▄▄▄▄▄▄▄▄

1. Charles Peguy, *Oeuvres poétiques complètes* (Ed. La Pléiade), pp. 484 and 571.

Perhaps it would be more realistic to analyze how charity can be married to our primary instincts—to the instinct of *preservation,* the *sexual* instinct, the *social* instinct, the *religious instinct* and thus by sublimating to expand these instincts.[2]

Until such time, however, as a theory of the "general virtues" may be restored,[3] we can rely directly on those good old sign-posts, the Commandments of God, the "Ten Words," always valuable indeed and which possess the advantage over the virtues of setting us right in the dialogical climate. Undoubtedly they must not be subordinated to the demands of charity in order to introduce them, as such, into Christianity. The chasm between their negative formulae and the positive calls of the evangelical Beatitudes must be acknowledged, and we have no right to halt our Lord at these "Words" beyond whose limits he himself passed. But the domains indicated by the old Commandments can still serve very usefully to set our footsteps in the right direction. It is indeed a matter of the fundamental requirements of the Lord in our human lives. These requirements are traditionally apportioned between the two Tables.

The first Table—the first three Commandments—corresponds to the instinct for the sacred, to the religious instinct. What does this become in the law of Christ? Should the Christian, united to God through charity, be also a "practicer?" The word sounds unpleasant to susceptible ears: is there really an indispensable exteriorization of charity here? Is not worship a "useless luxury" today, especially when

2. Cf. A. D. Sertillanges, *La philosophie morale de saint Thomas,* Paris, 1942, p. 158, note.

3. According to the desire of Père de Couesnongle, O.P., *Lumière et Vie,* No. 13 (1954), p. 133; *Revue Sciences philos. et théol.,* No. 43 (1959), pp. 601-620.

people are so busy? If it is of any use, is it not, anyhow, of minor importance? "Believing but not practicing;" surely is this the indication of ... good Christians? Do we not, as a matter of fact, cut down the time given to prayer on days when work is heavy? Are we wrong? Does not charity take the place of religion?

Let us go further. Outside of the actions laid down by Christ and reiterated by the Church, is not every act of worship which tries to reach God from here on earth a kind of anachronism, a sort of simple human superstitious attempt, always more or less "magic," to inveigle God for ourselves, or like some security reflex which says: "I am carrying out the rites which will save me from hell?"

This is a serious question, of which the traditional formulation is as follows: What are the bonds which unite the virtue of religion, if virtue of religion there be, to charity?

Let *dogma* enlighten us once more (I)! We shall see the place of *religious mediations,* and especially of *liturgical* mediations in our morality (II), and we shall deduce from this, as usual, some practical orientations (III).

I. CHRISTIANS, A SACERDOTAL PEOPLE IN A UNIQUE PRIEST

The Vocation of Man, Consecrator of the World

The spirit has, of necessity, a vocation of praise in respect to the Spirit: it acclaims and adores him from whom it springs.

When the spirit in question is human, the spirit of an incarnate being, this praise requires to be displayed in his body and by him all over the world. "Glorify ... God in your body," says Paul (I Cor. VI, 20). We can also understand: Glorify God in this extended body which for you is the world to which you belong with every fiber.

Thus we find ourselves promoted to be priests of the Earth and of the Universe. "The heavens show forth the glory of the Lord"—let us listen! Whence is their voice?

"There are no speeches nor languages, where their voices are not heard. Their sound hath gone forth into all the earth: and their words unto the ends of the world" (Psalm XVIII, 4-5).

It is up to man to decipher this text and give voice to it! It would be meaningless for God to create the starry universe and the wonders of nature without destining them for someone who could discover therein his Glory and his Bounty, and make a return of these to him by actions of grace, thereby establishing himself in full communication with this Glory; someone, moreover, who is charged, by virtue of his intelligence, with being the orderer of the world, and with conferring upon it, through the work of his hands, new harmonies which will redouble his praise and his joy.

Christ, Priest of the whole world

Unfortunately, man has found his vocation to worship too onerous a burden. With Satan, "the spirit who always denies" (Goethe), he has refused this service, this "diaconia." As a result, this world which was made to sing the glory of God he has dedicated to vanity, that is to say, to an idol (in the Bible the "vanum," that which is empty, the idol which does not exist). For man does not reject his destiny to worship. He perverts it, but it takes its revenge. It compels him to multiply the idols which enslave him; those idols which call him today are Money, Pleasure, Progress at any price, Love without laws, Race, Power—all of them insatiable divinities. The perverse cult of them becomes the very worst of slaveries.

Thanks be to God he has recreated us and liberated us from idols in Jesus Christ. Assuming in perfection the vocation of man, Jesus lived his whole life as a worship of the Glory of God. He is our High Priest, the "perfect religious of the Father" (this is the central theme of the Epistle to the Hebrews). In virtue of his Sacrifice, because his infinite innocence reunites all of us, the whole of humanity and the whole world with it have been consecrated at one stroke, offered to the divine Glory and in such a way that this impatient Glory demands henceforth to "spiritualize" them, for the Glory which has pervaded humanity with the risen Christ desires to blazon itself across the world and make it share in his Paschal Transfiguration.

In Christ man gives glory to God

To the extent that man is assimilated into Christ dead and risen again, the perfect mirror of the divine Glory, to that very extent he will be able, in his own turn, to glorify God, to bring men back to the adoration of God, to make them once more the mirror of the glory of God.

In this sense it is a fact that all the religion of man is now fulfilled "through Christ, with Christ, in Christ," that is to say, that it is given to us wholly from above. There is no other sacrifice but his, no other prayer but his. But we must make this sacrifice our own. We must echo this prayer.

185

"There is a treasury of prayers, an eternal treasury of prayers. The prayer of Jesus has filled it at a single stroke; has completely filled it; has filled it infinitely ... that instant when he composed the Our Father ... the prayer which we shall for ever only echo.

"There is a treasury of prayers. Jesus filled it .... And he expects us always to refill it, something which has not been understood by the learned of the earth."[4]

"Do this for a commemoration of me ...."

"When you pray—and you ought always to pray—say, Our Father ...."

II. A MORALITY OF THE GLORIFICATION OF GOD THROUGH LOVE

The bond between charity and religion is henceforth so close that it produces an *osmosis* from one to the other. Is it possible to imagine Jesus offering to his Father anything other than a filial prayer, a loving sacrifice? "I ... have kept my Father's commandments, and do abide in his love" (John XV, 10; cf. X, 17-18: "I lay down my life .... This commandment have I received of my Father").

Jacques Leclercq writes with justification:

"The adoration of the Christian is an adoration impregnated with love and the love of the Christian towards God is a love wholly impregnated with adoration. In practice the one is inseparable from the other and the Christian can scarcely distinguish them."

----

4. Charles Péguy, *Le mystère de la charité de Jeanne d'Arc*, Oeuvres poétiques complètes, p. 158.

1. *An Adoring Love*

Is there not some antagonism between these two words: love implying *intimacy,* adoration implying *distance?* If I am truly united with God like one friend with another, like a husband with his wife, can it still be possible to speak of adoration? Does not this reduce the relationship to the level of the creature confronting the Creator, of the servant vis-à-vis the Master? To ask this question is already to answer it. While in fact we are established in the dialogue of love as friends, as sons, as spouses, we do not cease to be creatures. The completely free bond of love does not suppress the fundamental bond of creation. Even if God has established a bridge between heaven and earth through Jesus Christ, the abyss between the Creator and the creature still subsists: God remains the Lord. He is only all the more wonderful in that he calls us his friends. That cannot but redouble in us both our love for Him and an appreciation of his greatness.

The great, loving witnesses to the divine Glory

A sentiment which has most markedly characterized the saints (those Christian-types to whom we should always refer when we want to think about the Christian life) is surely that of adoration, of bewildered wonder that such a grace should be afforded us without merit on our part. All the saints appear as witnesses to the divine Glory.

Let us think of the Magnificat of the most holy of creatures: "He hath regarded the humility of his handmaid." Let us think of St. Paul who never ceases to be astonished at the grace of his vocation ("me, the least of the apostles"). Let us think of St. Augustine who brought into all Western

Christianity a profound sense of the Glory of God (*"noverim te, noverim me!"*) Let us think too of the Eastern Churches which have preserved so vividly the sense of the ineffable mystery of God, of his shadow: their theology can only falter when it speaks of God, so profoundly is it abashed before his mystery. The whole of the East has this sense of the nothingness of the creature before God which we find among such of our own mystics as a Ruysbroeck or a St. John of the Cross.

Nor must we forget, in our Western tradition, the strong religious current of the French school. According to the very brilliant distinction made by Jean Guitton, there is the "mentality" of the French school, and its "spirit;" the mentality bound up with a phraseology of the 17th century may seem irritating to us and overly solemn to Bérulle; but getting beyond this mentality of an epoch, we can and should share its spirit, its especially keen sense of the Glory of God, of the worship of God in Christ the Priest, "the perfect religious of the Father" according to the Bérullian formula.

The inner submission of love

A Christian whose charity is lively can become, should become, the intimate of God. Christ in person invites him to do so: "I will not now call you servants, but friends." The Christian will never, for all that, drop into good-natured familiarity with his God. There was bound to be a reaction, and rightly, in recent years (and the liturgical movement has contributed to it) against certain exaggerations which were considerably over-"democratic" during the years 1930-1940. Obviously Christ wished to be fully Man and to remain very close to us, but Jesus Christ, the Son of God, the son of Mary, can never become "my pal." We may not trifle with God, even if he is "God-with-us." Even with the bridge lowered through the agency of his grace, an infinite distance remains between God and us.

The two fundamental facts of the human attitude when confronting God have been extremely well defined by R. Otto: God is, for man, both the One who fascinates and attracts because His love is near; and the One who makes us tremble through his holiness. "Attracted" by the Lord, we withdraw before his transcendent mystery. Both movements come easily to terms with authentic love, for this—as is too often overlooked—is not only an "inclination towards" but a "distance from and respect for" the person.[5]

The Cross of Christ, the most moving and loftiest mark of charity and of the proximity of God in respect of the sinner, is moreover the most amazing sign of his transcendence and of his baffling ways. The Cross is a "scandal" the meaning of which can be provided by God alone, God who appears to us at once as "entirely personal and entirely remote."

In the most fervent Christian life, therefore, the sense of interior submission should always persist. God has loved us earnestly, we must respond to him with an earnest love which understands how to remain on its knees: this is one of the surest signs of spiritual health and Christian balance.

2. *A Loving Worship*

"And now, brethren, I appeal to you by God's mercies to offer up your bodies as a living sacrifice, consecrated to

---

5. Cf. B. Häring, *op. cit.* I, p. 114: "Individuals meet each other only in an attitude of both loving advance and deferential retreat."

God and worthy of his acceptance; this is the worship due from you as rational creatures" (Rom. XII, 1). Your "bodies" says St. Paul, but he means your whole selves.

Our communion with God is, indeed, in its formal reality, an immediate communion, spirit to spirit. But for corporal beings as we are, whose bodies are so often, in actual fact, far from docile to the service of our spiritual end, this communion can only develop by means of *tangible media*: external realities, words, gestures, the whole life of worship are the necessary sustenance for this communion with God. While it is true that creation requires the human voice in order to praise God, man too needs the realities of the world about him, of his body, of external gestures, as the *media of his inner adoration* and of his communion with God. These media, even though they will become dull, even confusing, at certain times, (not even excepting the liturgy and the sacraments), are indispensable if our adoration is to conform to our nature, placed as it is in time and space. For our feelings dwindle away without our actions, and our actions aspire to the fullness of external behavior.

The offering of the Mystical Body

A worship which is perceptible to the senses is all the more requisite in that we communicate with one another by means of the senses and in that God desires to be glorified also in the *Body of the Church*. This is one of the most solid and constant factors in the history of Israel. It was not a few Israelites only, certain privileged personages, who were the witnesses to God's glory among the nations. It was the People of God, the entire community of Israel. Today it is the Church, the true Israel of God, which, according to the First Vatican Council, constitutes "this sign raised among the nations" by which the greatness of God shall be recognized or which, through its unworthy existence, shall "blaspheme his Name." Now this Mystical Body incorporated with the body of the risen Christ, and which constitutes the most eminent sign of the Glory of God, could not proclaim the primacy of God, and the necessity for a ready service to "the glory of His Name" if side by side with private worship it did not have a *public worship,* a "liturgy," a work of the people as a people. To assume at specific times and places the outward appearance of the worshipper and glorifier of God, a liturgical appearance, is clearly one of the fundamental requirements of the mission entrusted to the Church.

Offering of the heart

Let us beware, however, of giving credit to corporal gestures in themselves and of reducing the liturgy to an external display. While this is an original feature of Christian morality it demands, what was so often craved by the prophets and definitively proclaimed by Christ, the primacy of the "heart" in all worship. To honor God with the lips is not enough, even if the praise is magnificent: this worship must be a living reality in the heart of the faithful, an adoration "in spirit and in truth" (John IV, 24).

Intimate devotion must undoubtedly be the spiritual truth of our external worship, the soul of our religious practices, but this in itself must be wholly impregnated by love, it must be *the harmonious adoration of a formal act of charity.*

"Just as the external Glory of God has its source in his intimate and eternal glory (that which the Father gives to his Son), so the virtue of religion in a Christian finds its

191

inspiration in charity: charity which, being a theological virtue and so having access to the intimate Glory, will make of this worship of the glory of the Father who reveals himself, a filial worship . . . .

"Without charity . . . one may indeed carry out acts of external worship, but there is no question of referring to these in terms of virtue or of religion, or even of truly valuable worship. St. Thomas has to say of religion that it is (or should be) *a protestation of faith, hope and charity.*

"So that there is no aspect of any act of worship for the Christian which is not at the same time also an act of faith, hope and charity."[6]

Thus charity inspires adoration and adoration expresses love.

3. *In Christ*

All this is achieved for us "in Christ" (an expression which occurs 164 times in St. Paul), in the "mystery of Christ" given from heaven, which both profoundly consecrates our religious obligation and makes all our methods of approaching the sacred very feeble. We no longer have to offer our prayers but his, no longer our sacrifices, but his sacrifice.

In the Death and Resurrection of our Lord

This is why our morality and our spirituality—"it is indeed the same thing" as Père Régamey would say[7]—depend

----

6. B. Häring, *op. cit.* II, pp. 142-143.

7. Cf. Père R. Régamey, *Notre doctrine spirituelle en face de l'esprit du monde,* in *Lumière et Vie,* 50, (1960) p. 46.

totally upon our baptism, the rite which is our initiation
into the death and the resurrection of Jesus Christ, our
entry into new life.[8]

It would be a good thing to indicate here that not only
our worship but our faith and our charity from now on
are dependent upon the whole sacramental system, for
God takes up our sacred signs and in order to come to our
encounter Himself makes them the instruments of the Passion and Resurrection of the Redeemer.

We must note how the whole liturgical life of the
Christian—and consequently his whole Christian life—re-
volves around Sunday, the Lord's Day, Mass Day, the Day
of Christ's Resurrection; we must extol this "mystique of
Sunday" and note how on this day—and moreover throughout all sacred liturgy as it unfolds through the course of
the year and of life—it is not we who are thus offering worship to God, but God who is lifting us up into the realm

---

8. While St. Paul recalls the wording of the Commandments in regard
to our neighbor (Rom. XIII, 8-10), it seems clear that the formulation of
the first Commandments, as inherited from the Old Testament, was neglected
by the primitive Church and could not be taken up again later on without
some alteration, since the Jewish ceremonial law was now out of date.
Christ, the incarnate image of the Father, had made unnecessary the
direction: "Thou shalt not make to thyself a graven thing, nor the likeness
of any thing" (Ex. XX, 4). This Commandment appears, therefore, to
be simply a repetition of "Thou shalt not have strange gods before me."
Hence the hesitations of the Christian Tradition in the composition of
these first precepts (cf. H. Cazelles, *art. cit.* col. 500).

In practice, just as the Commandments were the first beginnings of
the developments of the Jewish ceremonial law, their triple declaration may
be regarded today as the first beginnings of the directions of the Church
regarding the matter of worship. A recent (15th century) tradition
attempted to sum up the most essential elements in a list parallel to the
Commandments of God. These *Commandments of the Church* are subject
to variation and revision: they have been listed as four, five, six (the

193

of his glory as manifested in Jesus Christ and by the same action establishing us in the risen Church with him.[9]

In Expectation of His Return

The first Christians awaited the return of Christ on a Sunday (did he not appear in the Upper Room on Easter Sunday and then eight days afterwards?). Every one of our Sundays ought to be a preparation of this eternal "eighth day." Every one of our Masses, the profound essence of Sunday, ought to give vent to our desire that Christ may return. May "the times of refreshment" come (Acts III, 20)! "Come, Lord Jesus!" (Apoc. XXII, 20). The ascent of humanity towards the supreme Epiphany of God assumes that the Gospel of the Glory of God "in the face of Christ Jesus" will be preached everywhere (cf. II Cor. IV, 1-6).

Just as it would not have been suitable for the Messiah to come to Israel without his advent having been preached in advance, so too it must be that his return, which is directed to the whole earth, should first be preached to the whole earth. (And the perfect announcement is the Mass, "until he come," I Cor. XI, 26). When will this proclamation be completed? That is for the Father to judge. For us, who are desirous to "hasten the advent of the Lord's day," we are burning with the wish to preach this glory

---

usual figure), and sometimes even ten (cf. R. Brouillard, art. "Commandements de l'Eglise," in *Catholicisime*, II, col. 1337-1339). From all evidence they bring us back to *Canon Law*, from which they derive their authority and today they find their true expression in the different ritual Directories approved by the Church, universal or local.

9. Cf. Th. Camelot, *La spiritualité du baptême*, coll. "Lex Orandi," 1960.

everywhere and to make of it even now the new song on all lips and in all hearts.

III. CATECHETICAL AND PASTORAL ORIENTATIONS

Charity takes seriously this life which God has given us and which it is so good to give back to him. Charity requires us to promote a true worship of *body*, *heart* and *life*.

True worship of "body"

Only genuine earthly realities should form part of this worship. The liturgical revival has made us quite intolerant of false candles, artificial flowers, fake marble, "simpering" statues, over ornate, fussy music. Let us extend this need for truth to our actions of worship. Let us have no shams; let us not put on a show of praying, let us just pray; nor a show of singing, let us sing. The healthy normalcy of the human action is a guarantee of its religious value. Let us not think only about doing something which is *valid*, but of *value*.[10]

So too the faithful can understand why the radio and television are only imperfect approaches to taking part in the Mass; we must be *present together, genuinely physically* at the sacrifice of the Body and Blood of Christ. To be sure, this physical presence must not be that of a body rigid and uncooperative. We must enter into the action with our bodies—gestures and attitudes will then appear to find their culmination in the sacramental communion.

▬▬▬▬▬▬▬▬▬▬▬▬▬

10. A. M. Roguet, *Sévérité ou vérité dans l'administration des sacraments,* in *La Maison-Dieu,* No. 6 (1946), pp. 92-106.

True worship of the "heart"

For all that there is no question of disassociating the liturgy from the interior life. "He who sings, prays" goes the saying. Well, let him pray truly! Let his lips speak from the fullness of his heart. That is to say, let them express the profound devotion of a heart welling up with charity. This should not encourage us, nevertheless, to mutter endless prayers if they do not sustain our spiritual life, and should persuade us that the best prayers are not necessarily the longest.

Has not our doctrine of *ex opere operato* rather reduced the sacraments to effective formulae, however much heart we put into them? Here again the *valid* must not make us forget the *valuable*.

"To celebrate the mysteries of worship," said St. Ambrose, "is to find Christ again in his mysteries."[11] The risen Christ comes to us to renew with us his eternal Community. His is a hidden rendez-vous where He is always the first, where He always retains the initiative and recaptures us in the Holy Spirit, but where He gives us the opportunity to answer His call by the real gift of ourselves in charity, in truth of "heart."

True worship of "life"

The "liturgy of the temple" should provide for the religious orientation of all our human tasks. The "big moments" of worship are not intended to remain erratic periods lost in long intervals in our life: they must fix a new orientation of our whole existence. The liturgy does not come to a

11. *In prophetam David*, no. 58.

196

stop for us when we leave the church; *our whole life* must be orientated by it *"ad majorem Dei gloriam."* It must be in all its actions and in all its works a life dedicated *to the Glory of God.*

This same truth is theologically formulated in the saying that it is religion which makes the union between charity (and more generally the theological life) and the moral virtues, those which apply on the plane of daily human activities. In other words it gives to the whole moral life *a religious form:* all earthly tasks, on the level of creation, receive a religious consecration from it; as it has come from God, creation returns to God, after having fulfilled its earthly function *as a service in his praise.*

This revaluation of the virtue of religion is particularly necessary in a world where the temporal (through technology) is always more blatantly asserting its importance and where man, losing his awareness of his condition of creature, is in danger of becoming laicized. Laicization is all the more formidable in that there is a certain normal autonomy of the temporal. Under such conditions certain people may be tempted to feel that liturgical action has become to a great extent useless—or at least that it has only a minor importance. It is essential that the exact opposite be vigorously asserted. The more the Christian is involved in the business of the world, the more must his life of worship be truly intensified. That alone can inspire a religious soul in the course of its earthly tasks and help it to fulfill them in terms of God, in the warmth and light of charity.

Provided that *life* be present in prayer and in worship, then worship and the charity which inspires it will in return inform the whole life and make it an answer to the vastness of God's love.

197

CHAPTER TEN

THE LAW OF CHRIST IN HUMAN RELATIONS

There are certain teachers who might object that we boast of the uniqueness of Christian morality and claim that it can be summed up in charity. "Is it possible," they ask, "to teach the catechism—the whole catechism—from this standpoint?" To this we reply, Yes, certainly. It is simply a question of summing-up morality at the level of inspiration and motivation—the Christian should do everything for love of God. But one cannot be content to repeat this indefinitely. The interesting question is: starting from charity, how does one collate with justification the entire content of text-books of morality?

Well, we have already outlined the answer. *Charity in relation to God,* through the virtue of *religion* which the respect inherent in love assumes, includes the *first three Commandments* and therefore all the activities of the religious life. So too *charity in relation to our neighbor* must, through the intermediary of justice, an inherent requisite of love (justice blended of other moral virtues which assist it), govern the *remaining seven Commandments,* and therefore the various activities demanded by the multiple realities of this world.

But this parallel should not give rise to any illusion. Charity in relation to God and charity in relation to our neighbor are, as we have already said, only one and the same love, and that not a human but a *divine* love. It is *His love* which God gives us. What is more, and we would like to emphasize this because it is less heeded, just as religion in the logic of charity towards God pursues the glory of God, so true justice, in the logic of charity towards our neighbor, pursues the glory of man, that is to say, his power and the harmony of his relationships. Only, in the final analysis, this glory of man is a *divine* thing. It is indeed in this that God places his glory according to the saying of St. Irenaeus, *Gloria Dei, vivens homo.*[1] Then the organic unity of our morality is made truly apparent. It is not content to *assume* the facts of natural morality, such as those our conscience dictates and which we seek to reason out, it *enlightens* them from above. It justifies what it assumes.

"Far from underestimating the riches of human morality," writes Père Liégé with great insight, "to act within the faith cannot fail to *assume* them." But he adds: "At the same time, acting within the faith reinterprets them in a higher world of the evangelical motives where they are more decisively justified and amplified."[2]

In other words, the ideal is indeed, as we have so many times repeated, "that one should never dissociate the proposition of the faith in its dogmatic aspect from the proposition of Christian action which it implies."[3] Now of course this implication must be perceived. One may assert it in the name of the natural conscience whose utterances the Christian conscience ratifies. But one may also desire to bring these utterances into the open, to discuss them

---

1. St. Irenaeus, *Adv. Haereses,* IV, 20, 6. Cf. B. Häring, *La Loi du Christ,* III, p. 180.

2. A. Liégé, *Aux sources de l'agir chrétien,* in *Catéchistes,* April, 1961.

3. A. Liégé, *op. cit.*

in the light of the faith. This is one of the tasks of theology.

We shall try to show here, without, of course, being able to enter into detail, how a morality of charity involves the last seven Commandments and seeks to define their requirements. The *dogma* which places all earthly things in the glory of the Trinity (I) justifies the actual requirements of our fraternal *morality* (II) and orientates our *catechesis* and our *pastoral* approach.

I. THE GLORY OF GOD AND THE LIFE OF MAN

In corporal and terrestrial realities nothing escapes God's plan to establish everything in charity. The mysteries of the Trinity, of Christ and of the Church, allow no doubt of that.

The Trinity and Creation

In what way can the dogma of the Trinity really throw light on morality when this is a matter of man and of nature? Does not this bring us back to "God, Author of Nature," the one God whom our reason can know?

This is a fallacy which must be absolutely rejected. That reason fails to know, through its own efforts, the mystery of the Trinity does not prevent this mystery, when it is known, from throwing light upon the profound meaning of Creation. Creation is an echo of the mystery of the Trinity. The teaching of the Epistles to the Colossians and the Ephesians, the Prologue of St. John, and finally, the Credo, must be taken seriously when they tell us that *all* has been created *in Filio* (in the Son). Let us listen to St. Thomas:

"Admitting, according to the Catholic faith that Persons proceed in God identical in divine essence, a procession which is not demonstrable by reason, then it must be recognized that this divine, perfect procession is the reason and the cause of the procession of creatures."[4] And consequently: "The Father expresses Himself *and every creature* through the Word whom he engenders: this Word, in fact, adequately represents the Father and *every creature*. Likewise the Father loves himself *and along with himself every creature* through the Holy Spirit, for the Holy Spirit proceeds as love from the first act by reason of which the Father loves himself and *every creature*. It follows from this that the Word and the Holy Spirit have a relationship, quasi secondarily, with the creature."[5]

It is not certain that Christian thought has drawn all the consequences of this inclusion in some manner of the mystery of Creation in that of the Trinity. The glory of the world and especially that of man for whom the world is ordained (cf. Gen. I. and II) should be understood as an extension of the Glory of the *Trinity*. In other words, *everything works in a reciprocity of intelligence and love*. While God extends to us his own Trinitarian relationships by his grace, he comes to complete our nature truly, in this perfect reciprocity, by revealing to us that everything which this reciprocity dictates to us was already moving towards that end.

----

4. St. Thomas, *In I Sent.*, d. 10, q. 1, a. 1, quoted by E. Bailleux who adds: "It would not be possible to state more clearly the incidence of Trinitarian action upon the exercise of creative power. The creative act yields its deepest meaning when theological reason links it to the mystery of the Three Persons." (*Personnalisme de saint Thomas en théologie trinitaire,* in *Revue Thomiste,* Jan. - March, 1961, p. 39).

5. 1*a*, q. 37, a. 2, ad 3 um.

Christ and Creation

The mystery of the redemptive Incarnation, culminating in the Resurrection, bears witness to the end to which Creation leads, namely, perfect assumption into the glory of the Trinity, therefore into limitless reciprocity. It is the Risen Christ who can say: "Behold I am with you all days even to the consummation of the world" (Matt. XXVIII, 20).

"In my Father, who is my God and your God, I shall be present with you," He seems to say, "in a universal presence. My risen Body will no longer suffer hindrance. It is a *spiritual Body,* conqueror of time and space, *wholly a mediator of the communion to which the spirit aspires.* The divine Glory penetrates it, that Glory which is the eternal reunion of love of the Father, the Son and the Spirit."

The Church and Creation

This Body of the Risen Christ is the principle of the Mystical Body. It is in the Paschal splendor of Jesus Christ that we meet each other. It is very clear that nature, the body, the cosmos are not excluded from this meeting. They serve it. They are the fabric of it, and, because, as St. Paul tells us, they aspire to perfect freedom, they are the means of achieving the final passage into the Glory of the new heavens and the new earth. *Every time they serve charity, they progress in this sense.*

The fact that the ecclesiastical power is distinct from the civil power should not conduce to the withdrawing of what is "secular" from the control and the animation of charity. On the contrary it should be emphasized that the duality of powers, the generator of liberty, has for its aim a more *authentic* and more complete symbiosis of the divine charity in the most temporal provinces. Everything is for charity. "Whether you eat or drink, do so for the glory of God." To eat and drink healthily should assure life for man. But this life in its own turn is a praise of God. It is so quite especially through a reciprocity of the spirits whom the bodies must serve and which indeed is often expressed by meals taken in common.

In short, ALL derives from the charity of the Trinity and requires to be fulfilled therein.

II. A MORALITY OF THE ACTUAL DEMANDS OF FRATERNITY

The morality of charity, therefore, should govern everything in the terrestrial world. But how? How are we, starting from that point, to coordinate all the demands of our consciences with regard to the good use of the things of this world? The answer is that one must start from a principle—in this case the principle of *corporal inter-subjectivity*. There follows then the necessity for a guiding virtue, namely justice, the mediator of charity, and from it the series of *precepts* develop as so many positive factors of a human fraternal life.

1. *A Principle: Corporal Inter-Subjectivity*

It is not sufficient to say that humanity, in God's view, is a multiplicity of individuals polarized by an inter-personal communion in the unity of the divine charity which is to be found at the heart of the Trinity. It is necessary to have a clear understanding of the nature of these individuals. We are not pure spirits and we never shall be. Even if our Lord assures us that in heaven there is neither marriage nor giving in marriage, we know nothing about it except that the beatitude which has been promised is a *human* beatitude and not an *angelic* beatitude—the Risen Christ is in heaven with His glorified Body. We are subject to corporal limitations. Our communion can only be a corporal inter-subjectivity. No one can wish to ignore that without shirking God's plan "the man who pretends to act like an angel acts like an ass."

In other words charity must accept the mediation of the corporal realities. No one doubts that the new heavens and the new earth, in the likeness of the "spiritual" body, directly serve the communion of spirits. The corporal world must serve it here on earth. The morality of the last seven Commandments simply estimates the demands of this service.

2. A Guiding Virtue: Justice and Charity are essentially related

The common denominator of the demands imposed on the world of bodies for the service of charity is given to us through justice. Why? Because, in fact, while it is the terrestrial realities which serve the dialogue, which personalize and unite (we are thinking again now of the meals taken in common), there are others among them which divide, which depersonalize, which make superficial or which collectivize. This fact in itself requires explanation.

The opacity of matter

Whether we like it or not, bodies and terrestrial realities are *material*. The spirit proves their opacity straightaway.

205

Lovers dream of being transparent to one another: this is simply because their desire for absolute communion comes up against bodily density and opacity. Here we might quote Blondel's famous saying: "How strange is the solitude of bodies; and all that anyone can say of union comes to nothing in the face of the solitude they cause."[6] And does not wealth also create solitude? Who are the rich whose wealth is a mediation of charity? Is it not, more often, a wall of misunderstanding?

The weight of sin

It is also a fact that bodies and human realities, the necessary media for a personal communion, find themselves, as the result of sin, in a state of wretchedness and weakness. The human realities are good in origin and according to God's designs, but they are equivocal in the use that man may make of them on account of sin—they can serve the communion of individuals just as much as they can serve their *division in hatred and egoism*. In practice our personalities, because they are imperfectly reunified through grace in the world of the body and spirit, have to struggle against the pressure of an instinct to possess material things, an anarchic instinct, blind and totalitarian. This instinct— or rather these instincts—for the appetite for materal things is diversified in varied urges, should be ruled, ordered, graded, so that the good things which they pursue may work towards communion instead of working against it. It is of no use to try to achieve this in a purely negative manner by repressing these passions; it should be done in a positive way, by converting all human "values" into the occasions

6. M. Blondel, *L'Action*, p. 256.

and the means of exchange, of mutual recognition, help and love. For that charity requires a realistic "handmaid"—this it finds in justice.

"The Organization of Love"

Undoubtedly justice "inclines towards the division of mine and thine, towards the equality of what is due and paid, towards objectivity, the clear outlines of situations, the precise determination of a minimum below which one cannot drop without arousing the reaction of defense, the violent sundering of the links of love and the claims of the other."[7] It rules the kingdom where men oppose one another, are divided as individual strangers to one another. But *simultaneously justice has no meaning except in relation to charity.* "It intervenes in the domain of biological exteriority only to create a milieu where love may penetrate and live. Justice assumes a meaning only by allowing man to love: it respects possessions with a view to relations with the person. It is individualistic.... When cut off from charity it presses towards division and ceases to be a link. Ruled by charity it is careful of the rights of others but by the process of gaining a victory over the instinct for acquisition which is too readily mixed with egoism."[8]

Relying upon *strength* and moderation or *temperance,* which are its auxiliaries, justice, the servant of charity, is never a glacial imperative born of an egoistic desire for peace. While being very concerned to give everyone what is accruing to him, it is attentive not only to things which are exchanged and to their objective demands, but equally

7. G. Gilleman, *Le primat de la charité en théologie morale,* p. 301.
8. G. Gilleman, *op. cit.,* p. 305, passim.

to the requests and aspirations of individual persons. It wants to be, in the wonderful definition of Père Sertillanges, the "organization of love."

3. *The Commandments, Actual Channels of Charity*

Listing in detail the demands of justice is the way to make known the practical avenues of charity. Now St. Thomas teaches us that "the precepts of the Decalogue relate to justice whose acts they determine."[9] And Père Sertillanges confirms:

"The first three precepts of the Decalogue relate to the virtue of religion, which represents the highest justice. The fourth is relative to family devotion which comes in second place. The remaining six give the precepts of justice in the current sense, that which rules the relationships between equals."[10]

Order

How should one arrange these Commandments of the "second Table" to the best advantage so that one may see in them the ways of charity? The answer is, according to the importance of the exchanges which they govern.

As we are incarnate spirits our *relations* between human beings may be *more or less spiritual.* Certain exchanges, concerning health, or the integrity of the body, sexual love, material possessions, are the less spiritual ones. The more spiritual ones are those which cover purely the interpretation

----

9. IIa - IIae, 2. 122, a. 1 and 4um.
10. A. D. Sertillanges, *La philosophie morale de saint Thomas d'Aquin,* pp. 335-336.

208

of living words, or art under all its forms. It is necessary to underline the importance of the spiritual exchanges, (thoughts, feelings ... etc.), because they are the most personal and because all the other exchanges are at their service including human love which needs to deepen into spiritual friendship.

The Eighth Commandment

The first place must therefore be granted to the spiritual exchanges of the communion in *truth* and *beauty,* whose instruments are speech and art. Justice demands truth and beauty; but lying and ugliness may distort them. Hence the Eighth Commandment. The purely negative formulae of it, which are easier to grasp by morally frustrated people, are particularly well known through sheer habit: "You must not lie, and you must not bear false witness." But the morality, above and beyond this zone of sin, has an immense positive field which must be explored, this field where speech and art are sovereign: a morality of the techniques of communication must demonstrate how all this should serve the communion in charity, beauty and truth among men.[11]

The Fifth Commandment

Then must come the corporal relations, under their most elementary form: *corporal coexistence,* respect for the life

▪▪▪▪▪▪▪▪▪▪▪▪▪▪▪
11. Is it necessary to emphasize it? Each Commandment confines itself to the *principal* or rather to the *rudimentary.* So, therefore, when we go beyond the negative formulation of the precept, we must broaden its scope and include in its design the entire domain of which it gives no more than the simple indication: thus we pass from "You must not tell lies" to love for truth, and from truth to beauty.

of bodies and for their integrity. To communicate together in charity it is first of all necessary to exist and to coexist, to admit the living presence of the other and to adapt to it. We cite for example in this context, beside the classic problems of the Fifth Commandment (homicide, suicide, etc. ...) certain more original or more positive aspects: the *Christian conception* of health, of hygiene, of sport, the relationships between health and holiness, the problem of the struggle against suffering, the problem of euthanasia, the limits to experimentation upon man, etc. .....

The Sixth and Ninth Commandments

God, in order to perpetuate the human race, instituted the *communion of bodies* in marriage. Now a certain morality practically knows the Sixth and Ninth Commandments only under their negative form. Everything becomes perfectly clear and balanced if, when studying the communion of bodies in marriage, the emphasis is placed on the *Christian meaning of sexuality*. Then one sets apart the privileges of Christian virginity which, in order to anticipate our state of glorious eternity, realizes the personal communion in a higher form. A sexual morality which is nothing more than a "morality of sin," or which leaves virginity in the shadows, is depriving itself of its Christian balance, because it is a misunderstanding of the vocation of sexual living, which is, in itself also a form of charity.

The Seventh and Tenth Commandments

Then comes the exchanges of material goods. Man must be fed, clothed, housed, must share in communal expenses, etc. . . . The proper functioning of these exchanges is of the greatest importance to personal and community relationships. Their organization in the complex state of the modern world poses numerous problems: property and labor, the just wage, the just price, the economic regime, social justice, (capitalism? communism? . . .) All these problems form an integral part of morality, which requires that they be resolved in the light of a *Christian conception of the community of persons.*

The Fourth Commandment

There remains the Fourth Commandment, the import of which might be indicated under the heading of "The Bonds of Society." We have kept it to the end. There is a reality which we cannot by-pass here on earth, namely, power, authority. It was not God's will that our progress towards the eternal community should take place solely under the rule of grace and the interior law. There was to be also the rule of an exterior law and authority. Why? The whole meaning of the exercise of an authority is to ensure *order and harmony in the different exchanges which condition our fraternal communion* and of which the other Commandments give all the details in range. Power is the instrument, "the arm" of justice (itself the basis of charity in all these domains). The whole meaning of power is to ensure justice at the level of all these exchanges (on account of the complexity of the rights, the interests and the needs of each person) and thereby to serve charity by favoring the communion of individuals.

Power exists at the level of the *family* unit: it is even more necessary when it is a question of governing a *State;* and the *Church* also possesses her power. The social frame-

211

work of our morality calls therefore for a Christian reflection upon the powers and duties within the Church.

Advantage

While there is no question of restricting Christian justice to the negative formulae of these precepts, they have the advantage of inculcating in us the *religious character of our morality*.[12] Formulating the requirements of the virtue of justice they remind us that we do not have to pursue a simple perfecting of ourselves, but to achieve a religious response to God. Being the injunctions of the Lord, they assure us that, with an outlook of "responsibility before God," we can and must assume our earthly tasks, which are the media of our fraternal communion. St. Paul, indeed, has no hesitation in summing them up as the very expression of charity (Rom. XIII; Gal. V, 14).[13]

III. CATECHETICAL AND PASTORAL ORIENTATIONS

As scholars of Christian morality we must truly teach with charity not only towards God but with charity also towards our neighbor. But we would be betraying charity if we did not instill into its service the sense of realism, the sense of *justice* and the sense of *institution*.

----

12. That is why the *Catéchisme biblique,* while it often introduces innovations, continues to refer to the plan of the Decalogue (Part III), as does likewise the third volume of *La Loi du Christ* of which this article provides a guide in summary.

13. Cf. the excellent pages of B. Sesboüé, S.J. *Si vous m'aimez, vous garderez mes commandements,* in *Christus,* April 30, 1961, pp. 192 et seq.

The sense of realism

We have never encouraged either remotely or specifically, we have indeed on the contrary discounted and repelled, the type of spirituality which consists in neglecting the most obvious of one's humble professional tasks in order to devote oneself externally to a multitude of "good works," or to cultivate piety at the expense of the duty of one's state. For all human affairs to sing the glory of God it is necessary that they exist, that they have their own consistency and density. It is necessary to take them seriously, to use them or to live with them—without getting caught by them—but also without angelism, without Manichaeism, without false scruples, in order to make them serve the glory of God in fraternal charity. According to the magnificent formula of the English poet, Coventry Patmore: "All realities will sing, nothing else." Our religious spirituality would certainly need, at times, to take *a course in realism* in order not to believe that everything is saved by the "good intention."[14]

The sense of justice

"Exceed justice so that the communion may come which completes all justice." The dictum is St. Augustine's. It says in fact that no one can stop short at justice—justice is at the service of charity. But before exceeding justice through the communion of charity, it is first necessary to complete its measure, "to accomplish all justice." There must be no naïveté in this sphere! It is no use rushing

14. Wise reflections of Père J. Y. Calvez, *Vie spirituelle et insertion dans le monde*, in the issue of *Christus* already mentioned, pp. 178 et seq.

through without stopping at certain points (the "connec-
tions") and thinking that charity will be enough to fix
everything! Hard reality, practical situations, human in-
firmity, all demand order, justice. *Anyone who desires to
be charitable does not despise justice.* He should even
desire one day to exceed charity-cum-mercy in a love of
equality. Again to quote St. Augustine: "You give bread
to someone who is hungry; and you gave to no one."[15]

The sense of institutions

By speaking ill of justice we should in the long run be
doing a disservice to charity. There is a similar error
which must be cleared up, namely, that which consists in
believing that charity, from the time it is institutionalized,
is no longer *personalist.* We have no hesitation in quoting
here a very fine passage from the Protestant philosopher,
Paul Ricoeur:

"The final meaning of institutions is the service rendered
through their work to people. If no person is drawing any
profit from them, they are vain. An institution revolving
for itself is a force which is turning over in a vacuum. But
this final meaning remains hidden. No one can evaluate the
personal benefits poured out through institutions. Charity
is not perforce to be found where it is displayed in a
charitable gesture: it is also hidden in the humble service
provided by post offices and social security. It is very
often the hidden sense of the social. It seems to me that
eschatological judgment would say that we will be judged
upon what we shall have done for people, even without
knowing it, by acting through the channel of the most

---

15. *Tract. in Joan.,* 8, 5, P.L., 35, col. 2038.

remote institutions, and that finally it is the point of impact of our love on the people we treat as individuals which will be decisive: 'I came to the post office and you served me as a person!' This is what is amazing, for we do not know when we reach individuals. We think we have achieved immediate love in close relations (man to man, hand to hand) and perhaps it is here that we are deluding ourselves: our charity is only moral exhibitionism. We think that we have not reached anyone in the remote relations of work, of politics, etc... and here perhaps it is that we have served and encountered our neighbor. The criterion of human relations would be to know if we are reaching people; but we have neither the right nor the power to apply this criterion. In particular we have no right to use the eschatological criterion as a procedure permitting us to give preference to the close relations at the expense of the remote relations, because, in actual truth, we also exercise through them a charity in respect to individuals, but we do not know it. Our charity here on earth is covered with the sociological cloak of history."[16]

Now one may understand that the "consecration of the world" of which the martyrology of Christmas speaks, the "mark of Christ,"[17] as Pius XII said, the seal of the Glory of God which must be always more plainly printed upon the world, is "essentially," according to Pius XII again, "the work of the laity themselves, of men who are intimately mingling in the economic and social life, participating in government and in legislative assemblies;"[18] because it is

16. P. Ricoeur, *Le socius et le prochain*, in *Histoire et Vérité*, p. 217.

17. Pius XII to the Second World Congress of the lay apostolates, *Documentation catholique*, 1947, col. 1423.

18. Pius XII, *ibid.*, col. 1417.

a matter, in the final analysis, of placing at the service of charity all the resources of man and of the universe, of making of them temporal media of Christian fraternity, through the *promotion of a harmonious civilization which may materially serve charity.* Teachers of morality, we must not then forget that its final technical determinations escape us and that "it is by the media of the conscience of the layman that the divine law is inscribed in the terrestrial community."[19] It is our job to give the sense of this responsibility.

19. *Directoire pastoral en matière sociale,* No. 32.

CONCLUSION

"One certainly cannot reproach the priests of this century with lack of devotedness: perhaps occasionally one might *reproach them with a lack of message* ....

"The incipient disaffection which we note in many places in respect to the Paschal vigil would seem to point to the fact first of all that we are still far from having preached the Mystery of the Resurrection to our parishioners as it should be preached ....

"Along with Dom Lambert Beauduin I think that, on the whole, the traditional rites of our Paschal vigil correspond with the anticipation of the believer of the 20th century, on condition, however, that he himself agrees to fulfill his task and to exist. *To exist, in this context, is to accomplish the passage from the supernatural sign to the Mystery.*"[1]

To the words of a pastor of souls who is most attentive to the world of today, it might be permissible to add that this "existence" in the Paschal Christ is existence according to the LAW OF CHRIST. An additional proof, alas, that "we have lacked message" is surely the very poor quality of our moral catechesis and the inadequate awareness that Christians have of being "sacramental men" dedicated to the vocation of "existing and living" in Christ.

We make bold to take again the road of the Fathers of

----

1. Daniel Pézeril, *Le mystère pascal et l'homme d'aujourd'hui* in *La Maison-Dieu* 68 (1961) p. 202, 196.

the Church so that ever more clearly our "morality" may take on the tone of the Good News of the Paschal Mystery. We have become, as the Epistle of St. Peter says, "a chosen generation, a kingly priesthood, a holy nation." The community of grace, confirmed and proved in the Paschal supper, should lead us to live as a Christian people, that is to say, to suffer with Christ, to die with Christ and to rise again with Him. While the already Risen Body of the Lord transmits his resurrection to our bodies which are still mortal when we receive him, *the law of the Body of Christ replaces the law of our bodies.* So we prepare ourselves in the same spirit for the Messianic feast of the end of time: "That you may eat and drink at my table in my kingdom" (Luke XXII, 30).[2]

---

2. Daniel Pézeril, *ibid.*, p. 201-202.

APPENDIX

The Moral Theology of Father Bernard Häring

THE LAW OF CHRIST

I. A CURRENT OF FRESH AIR BLOWS THROUGH MORAL THEOLOGY

"A definitive book," states Bishop Garrone in his preface.[1] And certainly its appearance marks an auspicious "date" in the history of the teaching of moral theology whose treatises and summaries were becoming extensions of Canon Law or *vade mecums* for the use of confessors.

It is true that there was no shortage of critics of these moral theology handbooks, which seemed to have lost all evangelical zeal and all enthusiasm for life and to have hardened into juridical formulae or lost themselves in sterile matters of conscience. The Kingdom of God, Grace, the divine person of Christ, the law of liberty and of charity in the Spirit no longer shone from their pages to transfigure them and endow them with dignity. The study of morality was not—how well I know it!—considered a pleasant oc-

---

1. To the French translation-adaptation of *La Loi du Christ* by Bernard Häring. Paris-Tournai. Desclée et Cie, 1957-1960 in 3 volumes. *Translator's note.*

cupation in the seminaries. And it was, in fact, a little of this "uneasiness," so gloomily endured, which urged Father Häring first of all to want, and subsequently to write, a completely new synthesis capable of firing seminarians, and a great many others besides, with enthusiasm.

What in fact could inspire greater enthusiasm than the Christian life proceeding directly from the evangelical "Good News?" What moral health and apostolic zeal were to be found among the Christian generations of the first centuries who lived quite simply "in Christ" as St. Paul had taught! This was the splendid "Christian morality" contained in the wonderful letters of a St. Ignatius of Antioch. Theology, I know, has reflected since upon the sources of Revelation and such reflection was essential; it has systematized these precepts of life; and we have had the moral section of the Summa Theologica of St. Thomas. Truly founded upon God, the source and the model to whom the creature, fashioned in his image, must return, enlightened by the example of Christ Who is the way of truth and of the return to God, this authentic moral theology looked promising.

What happened afterwards? It would take too long to go back over all that here. One may read in the first volume those pages which retrace the great stages in the history of moral theology. Was Christian morality to become a morality for the "sickly" and the "dying" in the spiritual life, or for those whose only ambition is the legal minimum which excludes all risk, all uneasiness, all eager search for the will of God and all personal "discovery of self, whereas all the time it should be an art of "living as a Christian"[2] and a treatise on Christian holiness?

---

2. Title of a work by Père Liégé in the Collection *Je sais, je crois.*

On all sides the urgent desire was being expressed that there should be a *more positive* presentation of Christian morality, a presentation more attentive to the *problems of our times* (which are not all new problems but very often just presented in a new context or in new terms), a presentation retaining *a more plainly biblical and evangelical flavor,* a presentation not solely for confessors and possessing only a vision of sin, but for the whole Christian people called to holiness in Jesus Christ (cf. Eph. 1, 4). One of the authors of these previously mentioned *"vade-mecums"* for confessors actually admitted a very few years ago, at the close of his own introduction: "It is my most ardent desire that there will be many authors who will not be content with simply providing suggestions and explaining how Catholic moral theology should be presented, but who will contribute to the task of presenting it with intensive and positive labor." This was a most revealing wish coming from an author who himself was considering "Catholic moral theology" purely from the angle of obligation, of the tribunal of penitence and of Canon Law. It is the desire which Father Häring's work should be able to fulfill.

However, though this work is the answer to the wishes of professors of moral theology, the benefit of such a renewal should pass very far beyond the circle of specialists and the milieu of the seminaries, should reach all the cultured laity, should reach especially the *catechists.* Though these will certainly never have to teach *ex professo* a systematic treatise on Christian morality, they will *have to provide the true orientations of life upon all the problems which confront the young people of our times.* "The Law of Christ" should be very valuable in enabling them to present the Christian attitudes of today, attitudes at once candid, positive and demanding in the most differing and

221

most exciting domains (often also the most dangerous by reason of their very ambiguousness)—the body, health, sport, work, the quest for truth, the joy of knowledge, art, modern methods of communication, the promotion of the Christian economic order and, in a most profoundly supernatural quarter, the personal vocation, the obligation of the apostolate, and so on . . . . This is merely a foreshadowing, in rapid and extremely brief outline, of the rich possibilities proffered by "The Law of Christ" for producing a whole "Christian style" of living, through occasional reflections, more elaborate catechisms, or even through the exchange of views, study circles . . . and gatherings of parents.

We may add without hesitation that a very great number of its pages are suitable for providing substantial *spiritual reading* and for nourishing the *personal meditations* of catechists. I am thinking, for instance, of such a chapter as that on the Glory of God, on the theological life or on conversion . . . and of many others. But here and now we are going to set out in more precise form the excellences of Father Häring's work.

II. SOME OUTSTANDING CHARACTERISTICS OF THIS NEW SYNTHESIS OF MORAL THEOLOGY

1. *A morality which does not artificially separate what should be joined*

Morality in this work is not cut off from doctrine. It is "a morality of the Credo," in the happy phrase of Bishop Garrone, in which the dogmas, which are not pure abstract statements but living mysteries (the Trinity, Christ dead and risen again, the Holy Spirit, the Church, Christ's Body, the Second Coming), engender life and demand a specific Christian attitude which has nothing at all to do with the morality of the hero, of the wise man or of the good citizen. "In the last quarter of the 16th century morality became, in the minds of a large number of writers, a separate domain, withdrawn from the direct and constant influence of dogma," states Congar. After this too lengthy and disastrous "divorce," here at last, we hope, the "indissoluble bond" is solidly renewed.

In particular, Grace and Morality no longer pursue their separate ways. The Law of Christ is a law of Grace, and this is not an impersonal grace (a kind of fluid emanating from God), but a network of relationships with living persons. It is the benevolence of the Father who calls us and saves us in Jesus Christ through the Spirit of Love. And grace is always first—we are primarily *a new being* (called habitual grace) *in Christ;* this new being of grace arouses *new action in the wake of Christ* and makes possible *a free cooperation* on our part. It is not we who make ourselves saints "by sheer brute force;" the Christian saint could never speak of "his justice, which is of the law" faithfully observed (Phil. III, 9). ". . . it is not of him that willeth, nor of him that runneth, but of God that showeth mercy" (Rom. IX, 16). It is "by the grace of God, I am what I am" (I Cor. XV, 10).

Finally one has here a *handbook of morality which is at the same time a treatise on spirituality* in the strongest sense of the word. Morality is spirituality for the very simple reason that He Who engenders it in us is the *Spirit* of Christ who is leading us ever higher in the wake of Christ. To want to reserve "spirituality" for a separate treatise is to deprive Christian morality of its highest manifestations. It is to give credence to that much too common error that holiness is something quite different from morality, that it is reserved to a small number of candidates, that there are two destinies, so to speak, offered legitimately to the Christian, namely, the security of the general laws or the "adventure of holiness." The evangelical outlook is quite different. Holiness is not a counsel—it is a common vocation (even if the methods of promoting it remain in the status of "counsel").

2. A morality of a wholly biblical "climate"

Father Häring constantly extracts from the Bible (from the Gospels and the apostolic writings especially) the light of the divine Word which illumines each question (these are the "biblical preludes") and the "governing principle" for the construction of his treatise, namely, that "religious" idea of *a morality in form of "dialogue" with the divine Persons,* in which man, who has been called, becomes the respondent of God and establishes with Him a "society of love" opened widely upon his fellow men. God becomes Someone for me, I truly become someone for him; invited, called upon, I must provide an answer which involves my destiny; I must respond practically to this last call of God, namely, Christ Himself; I have to enter into dialogue, at the heart of the Mystical Body, with all those who, like me, say "Our Father." In short, our morality could not be better defined than as *"a morality of responsibility in Christ."*

But the wonderfully full meaning of this formula should be properly grasped. It is all religion, all the community which it conjures up, this new community sealed by the Blood of Christ, and our response is integrated in it. It is a morality which is rigorously religious and which of course, like all morality, claims to govern our habits and our activities, to make us attain the perfection of our nature and happiness, but which, repudiating that merely superior form of self-seeking where one remains one's own center of reference, consecrates the entire life of man to the glory of God. *Christ rescues us from a mortal autonomy.* He places us in dialogue with the Father, with our brethren (his brethren), for he is in person the dialogue of God-Man: "In him all the promises of God become certain; that is why, when we give glory to God, it is through him that we say our Amen" (II Cor. I, 20). The perfect and consubstantial image of God, He restores us according to that image and original resemblance which we had lost. He becomes the living example upon whom we may model ourselves, our supreme norm. He gives us his Spirit to be the maker of this interior imitation for us and to make us live as sons, as he did; finally he leads us to the Father, into the Kingdom.

Here again in the *Kingdom of God* we have a pre-eminently biblical idea by means of which Father Häring collates the intuitions of that great initiator Hirscher.[3] It is a very biblical idea, and one which is also full of implications of a community, capable of making the idea of "the last end" more practical and more dynamic, and of purging it of every whiff of egoism. "To attain one's salvation" is no longer then a solitary and narrow concern, but a vast fraternal enterprise inspired by enthusiasm, and heaven becomes the banquet of all the sons of God in the Kingdom of the Father. What more beautiful image could be found to express that "society of love with the living God" to which humanity is called?

▰▰▰▰▰▰▰▰▰▰▰

3. Cf. also the recent *Précis de Morale chrétienne* by J. Steizenberger, Paris (Desclée) 1960.

3. *A morality which assimilates the best of current philosophy*

Philosophy, whether one likes it or not, is the echo (meditated upon, reflected upon, systematized) of the ideas, the cares, the worries and the problems of an era. A Christian morality which is sufficiently open and sure of itself to assimilate these without denying any of its own traditional values cannot fail to gain both in following and in effectiveness among our contemporaries. Would anyone object to that?

So "The Law of Christ" owes much, and its author makes no secret of it, to the *phenomenological current*, especially as found in Germany. And this is so much the better if it can give us the taste for inclining towards what is living and real, rather than towards theses enunciated once for all time and never afterwards brought into contact with reality. One chapter in the *first volume* is visibly inspired by the *philosophy of values*, a philosophy quite ready to receive, in its normal extension, the supreme and personal Good as a final Value. *Depth psychology*, prudently used where its results have been undisputed, allows of more enlightenment upon many questions which remained very obscure (unconscious motivation, liberty and psychic troubles...). It is, however, from the philosophic trend of *Christian personalism* that "The Law of Christ" borrows analyses most freely, along the lines of thought of a Mounier, a Madinier or a Jean Lacroix. The best pages devoted to relations "individual—person—community," or to the pair "justice-charity," owe much to *"Conscience et Amour"* or to any such work by Lacroix or Madinier (I am speaking of the French adaptation, the only one of which I can judge). And I think, for my part, few of the philosophies are so "naturally Christian" as personalism. A St. Thomas certainly experienced more difficulties in utilizing the themes of Aristotle!

The utilization of contemporary philosophy does not involve, moreover, any contempt for the *"classic" philosophy* of the Church, that of *St. Thomas*. Even though the author does not, for his own part, follow a Thomistic route (last end and beatitude, human acts, law and grace, the theological virtues and the moral virtues) he refers to the authority of the Angelic Doctor more than to anyone else, and the opinion of authentic Thomists like Maritain and Gilson is perhaps more often quoted than that of a Scheler, a Mounier or a Gabriel Marcel. Does that mean that all these philosophic currents are so perfectly assimilated into the moral synthesis of Father Häring that one can no longer distinguish the mark of the grafting? Well, that would be saying a great deal. However, this should on no account give an impression of related and unrelated pieces, and I think that St. Thomas would not disown an equal effort of intelligent eclecticism.

Sometimes one has even an impression that the *conjunction of biblical thought and more modern thought* can open up rich perspectives. I am thinking of a chapter in the first volume on "The Heart" which deals with human activity. Obviously nothing is more biblical than this conception of "the heart" as the source of thoughts, desires, actions, for good as well as for ill, a kind of "moral organism" if I dare put it that way. The "heart" reflects the profound intention of the spiritual being. Is he good or bad, circumcised or uncircumcised, as the prophets, and after them St. Paul, expressed it? That places us at our exact value and judges us in the eyes of Him "who sounds hearts."

The "moderns" come back to this idea of *a vital knowledge which involves the whole being*. The heart was even for Pascal that superior and intuitive intelligence wholly penetrated by spiritual love, which grasped truth and the highest values (especially God and the supernatural). His celebrated definition of faith is well-known, "God revealed to the heart," and so close to the basis of the evangelical formula, "Blessed are the clean of heart for they shall see God." Nearer to our own times *Max Scheler* finds again these depths of "the order of the heart" or of charity, of the philosopher of the Pensées. It is the "heart" which knows the moral law, for the knowledge of the law is not a simple item of conceptual knowledge, without attraction, without dynamism. It is a "cordial" knowledge, a spiritual "taste" which moves towards values and especially towards those of good. And the *intention of the good "heart" is to manifest itself in concrete activity*, genuinely in contact with reality. It could never be a substitute for action or a useful refuge for people full of ineffectual good intentions. Better still, it is by realistic activity, in contact with the world for its betterment, by giving himself to God and to others, that the moral subject expands his own personal value. Without aiming expressly for that it comes as an extra, "upon the back of action" as Max Scheler says.

It is clear that there is something virile and constructive in such a "morality of the heart." This is no matter of sterile intellectualism nor, on the other hand, of the sentimentality of people like Rousseau, nor again of the moral purism at which Péguy mocked while he wrote furiously: "Kantism keeps its hands clean by not using them." It is a matter of a knowledge of good which may already be an urge towards good and which can be expressed through an authentic labor for charity.

4. A morality "for our times"

Let us be clear that we are not speaking about a new casuistic morality, strictly limited to the problems of our times, uncertain of its principles which are being constantly called into question. Such an "opportunist" and dated morality would not last long. But let us recall St. Paul who, while solving with pastoral zeal actual and burning problems, found a method of formulating his solutions in a way which has lost them nothing in current applicability. Why did he do this unless it was because he met all the facts and actions to be judged with the pure light of the eternal Gospel, of examples of Christ and of the great law of charity. Conversely, in our days so that Christianity may not appear obsolete and without practical import, its revealed principles, clearly recognized and released in all their compelling force, should come to help the men of our times to "live as Christians" in a world which has evolved considerably since the times of the "Institutiones morales." It is a world of technology, of material comforts, of the cinema and television, but it is also a world of under-developed countries which, like a proletariat on a world scale, are well aware of the injustice of their poverty, and also of their strength. It is a world in which Christians are in the minority and should yet play their providential role of being the yeast.

We shall not be surprised, then, to find brought up and even studied at length, very modern questions such as art in the light of morality, the techniques of communication (for their excess can become "a menace to spiritual autonomy"), sport, experimentation on man, birth-control, help for the underdeveloped countries, de-colonization. It must be admitted, in fact, that the whole progress of scientific knowledge of man and his world leads to an enlargement of the moral consciousness, confronted by new perspectives. New possibilities are offered to our freedom of action, therefore to our moral choices. And this is why (especially in the course of the third volume) the author refers so often to the *authority of Pius XII*. No pope has more frequently nor more effectively exercised his role of moral guide of mankind and witness to the universal conscience. He is the perfect example of that pastoral solicitude which is concerned to enlighten all the personal steps in a world of continual movement and invention where it becomes continuously more difficult to find the just response to the call of God.

5. A *"new" moral synthesis according to the schema of the Ten Commandments*

God alone knows whether anyone has meditated, during these last decades, upon the "old" morality of the Commandments. Yet it is not by reason of a taste for paradox that Father Häring chooses quite deliberately to detail for us his "special morality" (second and third volumes) according to the schema of the Commandments. It is because the "new law," in spite of being *new*, remains a *law*. The precepts of the Decalogue have not been abolished—they are interiorized (the "heart," the Holy Spirit), assumed and unified in charity, but their obligatory force remains quite untouched.

It is true that they will give place, among badly educated or ungenerous souls, to regrettable "deviations:" there is a danger of legalism, even under the new law, a danger of considering only the negative aspect of the law, its constraining side, its limiting qualities, by confusing the morality of the Commandments with the morality of sin. But a morality according to the precepts retrieves its attraction and its dynamism when one recalls:

— that the Ten Commandments *come from the Lord* (they are "the Ten Words" as the author loves to call them);

— that *they are graces* and pedagogical helps which it would be presumptuous to think we shall no longer need some day;

— that the Christian keeps them through the interior inspiration of the *Spirit* and the fervor of *charity* rather than in order to "fulfill his duties." He loves them as did the fervent Jews (cf. Ps. 118) for, far from being a heavy burden, they dilate his heart;

— and that this love, following Christ, opens the way to *limitless demands*. In an evangelical climate one is very far from seeking the minimum which must be observed so that the juridical forms may be kept; this is rather a law of the maximum and of indefinite progress ("to love with our whole hearts, with all our strength, as Christ," "the charity of Christ urges us"). In short, these are not "laws for a minimum" but "commandments for a purpose" with limitless perspectives, in response to the calls of Christ. The Decalogue is not any longer a "frontier" bounding dangerous territories or a "line of death." It is a law of life and holiness.

The author is not against the morality which follows the schema of the virtues. He simply prefers the schema of the Commandments which has the advantage, as shown by what we have just said, of clearly emphasizing the priority of the divine initiative. It is God who calls, it is his Will which makes law (not an arbitrary law as Ockham and the Nominalists thought, for it is a loving Will), and man does not have to "invent" the good—he responds, and his response is, in part, a gift from God. It is precisely here that Father Häring brings in the virtues as those stable interior dispositions which allow us to fulfill the Commandments, which raise us (especially the infused virtues) to the level of the divine order. Is not charity, for instance, first of all a *precept* (the unifying precept) which it is not in the power of man to carry out in its fullness ("to love as Christ loved") but which the infused *virtue* of charity (infused into us by the Spirit) will allow us to practice? "The virtues should not be considered as the property of man nor the exclusive merit of his activity, but as an inestimable gift from God, as a permanent call to respond to God, and a permanent faculty to do so, not through a simple and particular act but through firm and durable dispositions tending to give always to the demands of the religious and moral life the response of love and of obedience." (1, p. 97).

At this point, it seems to me, the Commandments and the virtues are brought together to promote a life of holiness.

Finally, the author has a most effective way which is quite *positive* and, as it were, elevating, and which clearly reveals a new spirit, of exploring the matter of each Commandment. To be sure we must not lie, must not kill or wound, must not steal nor be guilty of injustice... but this is hardly calculated to develop a progressive outlook or to infuse any élan into life. Listen now to the titles of our author's chapters or sections, so different, so constructive and so attractive: "The positive requirements of charity" (where it is a question, among other things, of fraternal charity in the work of the apostolate); "Communion in truth and beauty" (this is the Eighth Commandment); "The Christian and health" and then "The Christian and

232

death" (Fifth Commandment); "The Christian meaning of sexuality, Christian marriage, Christian virginity" (Sixth and Ninth); "The Christian significance of material goods" and of their "just disposition," and "Outline for a Christian economic order" (Seventh and Tenth). All this rings out frank and clear, and, contemplating these great vistas, or rather these vast sectors of our lives and of our concrete activities which have to be Christianized, we can feel a taste for adventure approaching, for the lovely "adventure of holiness" and the entrance, on the breath of the Gospel, of an ardent and pioneering soul.

III. THE WHOLE MORAL LIFE OF THE CHRISTIAN IN THE RADIANCE OF THE THEOLOGICAL VIRTUES AND THE VIRTUE OF RELIGION

But the essential and most beautiful thing has not yet been said. With the *theological virtues* and the *virtue of religion* we have now reached the "sanctuary" wherein the whole moral life finds its source and its decidedly "Christian" character. "Morality hangs upon the theological virtues, the expression of sanctifying grace or, in other words, of the divine nature participating in ours.... For the man who lives the theological virtues there is no more exclusively moral life (1, 347, 349).

1. *The theological virtues*

The theological virtues (which are, as it were, the new permanent faculties of our divinized life) adapt us to God's life and take us out of ourselves in order to "center" us upon God. They do not aim, of their own initiative, at the direction of the world nor even at our moral perfection. Their aim is to open the *dialogue between God and man* which will be completed in eternity. They are eternal life begun, intimacy with God already commenced: St. John dwelt very insistently upon this aspect of our Christian life. It is in the nature of the theological virtues to anticipate, to hasten on, so to speak, through the various stages and intermediary stops in order to fix upon God, their final object.

Having come away from sin, from the land of darkness where we were wandering far from God and destined for His "anger," here we are now, saved, endowed with the "power to become children of God." *Faith* enables us to cross the threshold of that theological life (faith-conversion linked to baptism) and continues to enlighten our entire existence. *Hope* reaching out towards that radiant end, sustains our pilgrim's march. It is like a "second-wind faith" for daily living, enduring, persevering, suffering, while waiting to possess the benefits which *Faith* has promised it. Finally, *Charity*, the greatest of the three, will not pass because God Who is its source has called us to eternal communion with Him. These are three pulsations of the same filial life, three fundamental attitudes, closely linked, through which we adhere to God Who is Truth, Beatitude, Love, "but always in and through Christ." "Faith makes of Christ our Light, hope makes of him our Way towards Beatitude, charity makes of him our Life" (1, 347).

Such is the special movement of the theological virtues, God himself. But we would note at once that a "pure" theological life, a "purely" contemplative life of direct and exclusive dealing with God in Jesus Christ, is impossible here on earth, for there are all our inevitable terrestrial activities and our relationships, our exchanges with other men. All that is providentially desired by God and must, thanks to the animation of the theological virtues, *enter into the dialogue with God.* "Since the theological virtues are accorded to the Christian in so far as he is a pilgrim here on earth, *homo viator,* his exterior actions, his earthly tasks, his moral conduct, all assume value as the response to God, as responsibility before God (1, 348).

To go further, even our relationship with God could not develop as a dialogue between equals. Our love, for instance, despite its intimacy, cannot claim to become the love of a "partner." A nuance of infinite respect, of reverence and, as it were, of withdrawal ("Depart from me for I am a sinful man") should always mark it and keep it within the "proper" limits which our condition of creatures and servants assigns to it. Since the Son did not fear to become through his Incarnation the "suffering Servant," so much more must the adopted sons be prepared to do so. In short, our love of God, in Christ and following Christ's example, must be "a love which adores" and "a love which obeys," a love which makes of all our activities a worship of the glory of God and a love which proves itself by its accomplishment of the Will of God. I lay stress upon this remarkable presentation of our Christian life which has the merit of gathering into a unifying vision the three virtues of *Charity* (and the whole theological life with it), of *Religion* and *Obedience,* the first assuming, shaping the other two, without on the other hand suppressing their own demands.

2. *The importance of the virtue of religion*

The virtue of religion, authoritatively studied by St. Thomas, is so important that theologians, without going so far as to make of it a fourth theological virtue, place it immediately next to the three leading virtues. Its role is to take up the whole moral life with its varied activities and bring it to God in a *movement of adoration and of worship,* to abstract it wholly from the profane in order to *consecrate* it; it is due to religion that everything on earth becomes the food of divine charity.

Following St. Paul, C. Spicq, quoted by the author, sees in "religion" the necessary form which our love as reconciled sinners must take, in response to the infinite charity of God in Jesus Christ. "What is the response required of men in the face of the stirring of divine charity? The Apostle formulates it in terms of worshipful gratitude: to offer one's body as a living host, holy and agreeable to God (cf. Rom. XII, 1-2). All the moral virtues which are enumerated afterwards are conceived as the offering of a sacrifice full of the action of grace and praise .... In response to the justifying mercy of God, man should pay a debt of gratitude; he satisfies this by adoration, the homage to God of his whole life, this spiritual liturgy being for St. Paul the profound meaning of the moral life."

To consecrate our lives and the world to the glory of God is truly the only concrete way, without illusion, which we as creatures have of loving God. To see only the divine side of all reality, the bias through which one may make of reality a homage to God, if necessary to detach from clinging and ambiguous reality the fragments of the sacred which it is holding captive—this is our work as kings and priests of a wounded creation which groans awaiting its deliverance by us. And this response of worship we make also in Jesus Christ and according to his example, He whose mission is to gather all together, to reconcile all in his Blood in order to make everything a homage to the

236

Father; He who never sought his own glory; He who crowned his life by a perfect *sacrifice* to the glory of the Father and who wishes to gather our offerings into the great movement of his own in order to carry us along with him into the eternal radiance of the Glory of God. "I have glorified thee on the earth... now glorify thou me, O Father... the glory which thou has given me, I have given to them" (John XVII, 4-5, 22).

And at the opposite end of this vast élan of "consecration" might we not say that sin, which in the final analysis is the refusal to love, is primarily expressed by a refusal to worship or, more precisely, by a wrong worship, a kind of worship of idols—of the world and its values, of money, of the body, of oneself and one's own glory? Sin is a refusal of love because it is a refusal of worship, so true is it that man is essentially "a religious animal." Aristotle did not know how truly he spoke!

3. *The liturgy and the sacraments integrated into moral theology*

Since worship in its important moments is chiefly expressed by the liturgy and the sacraments, it is not surprising to find these taking the prime place in this moral synthesis. This is a new achievement. It is true that previous treatises on moral theology have dealt with the sacraments—and sometimes at considerable length—but they have done so in a totally different spirit. They discuss them from the canonical standpoint of validity, or as new "duties" added to others, but not as an actual condition of all moral life. To place the sacraments "at the heart of life" is, in fact, to renounce the conception of morality as simply a

237

perfecting of oneself through personal effort, and to place oneself in the *sphere of influence of Christ* dead and gloriously risen. Since our moral life is primarily a theological life, a configuration, through the Paschal mystery, of Christ, it is Christ in person, actually at work in His Sacraments, Who alone can perform this miracle. Our human efforts of faith, of conversion, of flight from sin and of penance, of the apostolate, are always outstripped, stimulated and taken in charge by the grace of God which comes to us through the sacraments of Christ. Grace works upon them from within, purifies them, consecrates them and makes them worthy of God. Through the sacraments Christ changes us from inside and assimilates us into his mystery so well that our effort is no more than a humble response of *fidelity*—fidelity to the grace of baptism (faith, death to sin and a new life), to the grace of confirmation (testimony and apostolate), to the grace of penance (conversion), to the grace of the Eucharist (charity and unity)....

These sacraments received in the Church, sacraments which form the Church by a welding of the Mystical Body, make *community demands* upon us. "Whoever has received grace through the sacraments of community must know that he is assuring his salvation in the best way, if he considers the grace received as a *demand of apostolic charity* in respect to the community, especially in its most feeble members." (II, 189). And the author expressly links up the obligation of the apostolate (the first of the "positive requirements of charity," III, 105), with the sacrament of Confirmation, the sacrament of the responsibilities of the adult Christian who should concern himself with the reign of God and with the salvation of his brethren. With regard to the Eucharist, who does not note the *urgent missionary* call

238

which it presents to its participants? While the people of the "household" are all gathered together for this great moment of their worship in spirit and in truth, and for this slice of contemplative life anticipating the "eternal leisure" of the "fatherland," they are not so gathered simply to be all together or to forget for a moment the evil world and their brethren, the rest of mankind. Gathered around the Table of the Lord, they bring to it *concern for all "the others"* who are not there, they draw therefrom a generous charity, from it they move out into their various stations in life and their radiance will lead in the others who are invited to the banquet. At Mass "we recall the death of the Lord *until he come*," but also so as *to hasten the hour of the Return.*

And now come perhaps the most original and the most profound observations. There are sixty pages devoted to *"The Lord's Day,"* Sunday, the day of *Mass;* Sunday, the day of *rest* and symbol of eternity. All our work of the week should become, in its radiance, a consecration of the world to God and a preparation, a final orientation towards the eternal feast. The conclusion of this chapter should really be quoted at length. "Replaced in the general center of our lives, the Lord's Day, the memorial of the Resurrection, the day of Mass and the day of rest, appears as the essential actualization of our virtue of religion, inspired by the theological virtues of faith, hope and charity. It consecrates our whole life and primarily our work and our suffering to the glory of God by uniting them to the passion and death of Christ, but also to His Resurrection which will soon be revealed in us" (II, 364). The Lord's Day becomes thus "the sign of the Glory of God over our whole life."

4. *Justice, handmaid of charity*

If the second volume of "The Law of Christ" appears to fly at a high altitude above the daily problems which present themselves to "us fleshly creatures," this is but an impression. It was essential, in any event, to begin by placing man in his proper place in relation to God (son, but also creature and servant) and by defining the divine climate (the theological life, the life for the glory of God) in which all his activities should develop. This is, after all, the indispensable condition of a healthy humanism.

It has already been foreshadowed that the liturgy and the sacraments, far from separating us from earthly tasks, demand an involvement in apostolic charity. Just the same, this transition from the theological and liturgical life to the life of humble and active charity is not made without difficulty if it is to be well integrated. "The biggest and certainly the most difficult problem for liturgical piety," admits Bouyer, "is perhaps that which awaits us when we come out of the church after the liturgical celebration."[4] The exhaustive third volume is devoted specifically to providing us, by listing them in detail, with the demands of "life in fraternal communion."

In moral theology the habit was established of viewing all our duties properly considered as moral under the convenient heading (of Stoic origin; accepted by the Bible: Wis. VIII, 5-7) of the *four cardinal virtues* flanked, it is true, by their associated virtues. St. Thomas had well sanctioned the practice, but in the course of studying him too much attention had been paid to the process of classification and too little to the delicate analysis of each of these

---

4. In *La Vie de la Liturgie*, p. 315, quoted in II, 368.

virtues and to the unifying spirit which sustains the whole structure. Too often his wonderful and luminous phrase *"charity, the form of all the virtues"* has been forgotten (or rarely been given in full). And yet is not *prudence* "the eye of charity?" It is the evangelical and by no means hesitant virtue which discerns the will of God in the providential situation (the *kairos*) and finds its way to an active involvement in charity. "Are not the virtues of *temperance* and of *fortitude*, with all their retinue of associate virtues, wholly and entirely subordinated to charity?"[5] The function of *justice* is, in fact, to prepare the way for charity. Gilleman[6] has well defined it as "The moral virtue which makes us respect the person of our brother in Christ, at least in respect of his rights, with the object of ensuring between him and us the minimum of relationship necessary to a union of charity."

Here, in fact, is the principle which governs the third volume, namely, *"charity, the form of all the virtues"* (not, of course, to render them unnecessary but to animate them from within and to complete them), all the particular virtues becoming the necessary "links" of a charity which desires to take realistic form. Such an outlook is already fruitful for it shows in detail that the "queen of the virtues" is not a queen without a kingdom, an honorary queen enthroned at the top, but that charity effectively raises up the slightest virtuous action and confers upon it a royal dignity. There is something better still, and that is recognizing that fundamentally this "deposit" of virtues, these concrete branches of charity, bear a common name, justice (in the

---

5. The observation is that of a Thomist, Le Guillou.

6. Author of the authoritative book, *Le Primat de la Charité en théologie morale.*

broad and quasi-biblical sense of the word) and that they are in sum just the accomplishment under all different aspects (the Commandments) of the will of God.[7]

In an article[8] Gilleman thus defined the role of moral theology: "Moral theology has the heavy and magnificent task of proposing the concrete ideal of Christian living to the men of our time. Its work is to take hold of them, wherever they are, in order to lead them to what they ought to become, herein imitating Christ, endeavoring to remain close to him and to offer him as the concrete ideal." Was he thinking, as he wrote this, of "The Law of Christ?" We might say quite simply that his suggestions have been fulfilled.

I trust now that catechists, having perused these brief impressions of the result of my reading, will decide to make direct contact with the work. The best way to do this might not, perhaps, be through an interminable progressive reading. "The Law of Christ" is too vast a "country" and it might be better to approach it by some more accessible or more familiar "landing-place" (a "biblical prelude," the summary on the obligations of the apostolate, on conversion, on the theological life, on the sacraments or the Lord's Day ...), to establish there a solid "bridgehead," to extend that and then to set out on a methodical exploration. I myself took that course and found it served me well. This, however, is simply a suggestion. In any event, this work of discovery very quickly discloses its fruitfulness and "The Law of Christ" becomes an indispensable instrument of work and of reference.

7. For practical details about "these meditations of charity" see Chapter X.

8. *Morale chrétienne en notre temps*, in *Lumière et Vie*, No. 50, p. 55.